new Moroccan style

THE ART OF SENSUAL LIVING

new Moroccan style

THE ART OF SENSUAL LIVING

SUSAN SULLY

Photographs by JEAN CAZALS

Contributing Editor MERYANNE LOUM-MARTIN

Clarkson Potter/Publishers
New York

PAGE 2: *A hand-dyed and screened silk shawl, created by American textile artist Paige Hathaway Thorn for Ryad Tamsna, features motifs inspired by Moroccan carved wood architectural details.*

PAGE 3: *Diminutive tiles glazed in varying shades of turquoise. (Courtesy Amanresorts)*

FRONTIS: *A modern interpretation of a traditional Islamic flower-shaped fountain, this Italian marble basin overflows with roses in the courtyard of Riyad El Mezouar in Marrakech.*

PAGE 7: *Nut-studded nougat from the candymakers of Fez is almost as decorative as the ancient city's architectural details.*

See www.susansullystyle.com for complete recipes.

Published by Clarkson Potter/Publishers, New York, New York.
Member of the Crown Publishing Group, a division of Random House, Inc.
www.randomhouse.com

CLARKSON N. POTTER is a trademark and POTTER and colophon are registered trademarks of Random House, Inc.

Printed in China

Design by ELEMENT group

Library of Congress Cataloging-in-Publication Data
Sully, Susan.
    New Moroccan style : the art of sensual living / Susan Sully ; photographs by Jean Cazals; contributing editor, Meryanne Loum-Martin.
Includes index.
    1. Interior decoration—Morocco.   2. Interior decoration—Morocco—Influence.
I. Cazals, Jean.   II. Loum-Martin, Meryanne.   III. Title
    NK2087.75.A1   S85   2003
    747'.0964—dc21   2002153339

ISBN 0-609-61045-7

10   9   8   7   6   5   4   3   2   1

First Edition

To my father and mother, John and Elizabeth Ryan, and to my grandmother, Roberta Ryan,

who instilled me with wonder and wanderlust at an early age

S.S.

To my two loves, Marie Ange and Clara

J.C.

To my parents, Seyni and Nicole Loum, without whom the Marrakech adventure would never have existed,

and to Gary, Edward, and Thaïs for their creative support and loving patience

M.L.-M.

Acknowledgments

OPPOSITE: *Pattern on pattern is the essence of Moroccan style, as seen in Jaouad Kadiri's villa, where a divan upholstered in a contemporary fusion mix of Indian and Burmese textiles extends in front of a zellij-decorated wall.*

Gratitude is especially due to His Majesty, King Mohammed VI of Morocco, for preserving his country's historic structures and artisanal traditions.

Royal Air Maroc, Hertz Rental Car of Morocco, Diversity Excursions, Dar Tamsna, Jnane Tamsna, Ryad Tamsna, La Maison Bleue, Amanjena, Riad Kaiss, Riyad El Cadi, Villa Argana, Riad Mabrouka, Yacout, Comptoir, Riad 72, Gogo Ferguson and David Sayre, and Riyad El Mezouar all deserve many thanks for their generosity in providing transportation, lodging, and fine cuisine in support of this book. Thank you for your fine example of fabled Moroccan hospitality!

Thank you, Meryanne Loum-Martin, for your boundless energy, brilliant insights into Moroccan style, old and new, and extraordinary hospitality. Thank you, Gary Martin, for lending us the incomparable resources of Diversity Excursions. Thank you, Edward and Thaïs, for being you.

This book would not exist without the insight of textile artist Susan Virginia Hull, who knew I needed to go to Morocco and helped me get there.

Guide and historian Mohammed Bouftila, artist Abdelkhalek Boukhars, and actor and antiques dealer Ben Jelloun of Fez all deserve special thanks for helping me experience the beating heart of that mysterious city. Thanks, also, to all the others who helped me find beautiful houses in Morocco, including Brandon Vaughan, Michel Raphalen, Jacques Peltzer de Breteuil, Antoine Van Dorne, Jean Le Ventalle, Xavier Guerin-Hermes, Gilles de Kerhor, Stephane Atlas, and Stephen Angell.

My gratitude is extended to everyone who opened his or her home, hotel, restaurant, or kitchen to assist in the research and photography of this book, especially Dan and Ellen Kiser. Even though we could not include every place we visited in the book, we could not have made it without all of your help.

Thanks are due to His Excellency, Ambassador Herwig Bartels, for his work in preserving the textile arts of Morocco and to the Global Diversity Foundation for its work in preserving and promoting awareness of the crafts, architecture, landscape design, and garden history of Morocco.

I am deeply grateful to Jean Cazals for the beauty of his photography, his boundless enthusiasm for the world around him, and his sense of humor, which kept us all laughing even when we were exhausted. A very special thanks is due to Veronique Leplat, who served as the tireless photographic assistant on this project. I also offer thanks to my husband, Thomas Sully, who accompanied me on my travels and seized the day to create his own renderings of the beauty of Morocco in watercolor.

Finally, I thank my agent, Deborah Geltman; my editor at Clarkson Potter, Roy Finamore; his assistants, Lance Troxel and Jennifer DeFilippi; and graphic designer, Eric Mueller of ELEMENT group for bringing this book into existence. Thanks also to Sandra Gilbert for encouragement.

SUSAN SULLY

Thank you to Meryanne Loum-Martin, who was the key to opening so many doors in Morocco and whose help made this book possible. Thanks also to her wonderful family for their company and hospitality. I also offer thanks to Susan Sully, fabulous organizer, partner in adventure, and a great friend. We could not have made this book without the help of Veronique Leplat, my *fidèle* assistant. And finally, a special thank you to Morocco, a country that really gets under your skin, and its people, whom I dearly miss.

JEAN CAZALS

In addition to all those thanked above, I would like to make a special thanks to Susan Sully, for her desire and determination to make this wonderful culture of tolerance and peace better known in the United States.

MERYANNE LOUM-MARTIN

Contents ∽

12   Foreword by Meryanne Loum-Martin

16   Introduction

32   Elements of the New Moroccan Style

44   **FUSION**

46   *Refashioning Fusion:*
      Dar Tamsna

56   *Sensual History:*
      Dinner at La Maison Bleue

65   *A Connoisseur's Retreat:*
      Riyad El Cadi

72   *An Orientalist Fete:*
      Cocktails at Comptoir Darna

81   *Milan Meets Morocco:*
      Riad 72

87   *Gogo Maroc:*
      A Moroccan Feast on Martha's Vineyard

98 MINIMALISM

101 *Meditation in Gray and White:*
Dar Kawa

108 *A Celebration of the Senses:*
Amanjena

117 *Moorish Hacienda:*
Jnane Tamsna

124 *Stone Age Modern:*
El Cherquï

133 *Maghreb Minimalism:*
Riad Mabrouka

138 DELIRIUM

140 *House of Dreams:*
Jaouad Kadiri's Palmeraie Villa

148 *Moroccan Fantasy:*
Riad Enija

155 *Sleeping Beauty:*
Tea in the Glaoui Palace

162 *Tower of Sand:*
Ministero del Gusto

169 *Maghreb Mania:*
Momo Restaurant Familial

176 REPOSE

178 *Riad Retreat:*
Luncheon at Ryad Tamsna

187 *Modern Moorish Revival:*
Dar Andalusia

193 *Understated Orientalism:*
Riyad El Mezouar

198 *Enchanted Tower:*
Riad Kaiss

205 *Paradise Found:*
Villa Argana

210 Glossary
213 Shopping Guide
222 Index

OPPOSITE: *Contemporary ironwork marries the fluid lines of Arabic calligraphy with the abstracted floral patterns of antique Moroccan artisanship.*

Foreword

I CAME TO MARRAKECH FOR THE FIRST TIME IN DECEMBER OF 1985 and had the opportunity to start the project that became Dar Tamsna six weeks later. I discovered a place where I could walk along the ramparts of an ancient city suffused in a clear light that recalled the magic of Rajasthan. Everything within and beyond the city's walls was saturated with color: houses constructed from red ochre mud, green palm trees that lent the *palmeraie* outside Marrakech the atmosphere of a desert oasis, the dark blue twilight sky that ends in the snowy line of the Atlas Mountains. In Marrakech, I enjoyed dinners that offered a sensuous discovery of spices accompanied by a mesmerizing sound track of live music—sometimes Arab Andalusian, sometimes African. These meals were often served in the surreal atmosphere of old candlelit palaces where we sat in art deco chairs that had not been reupholstered since the French Protectorate.

Morocco's sensual feast is deeply and daily rooted in history. It is all about time and about sharing. Time, because things have looked, tasted, smelled, felt, and been heard the same way for centuries. Musicians played the same song many centuries ago, cooks prepared the same recipes, and poetry has celebrated the archetypal Islamic gardens since the Middle Ages. Time is also an important feature of Moroccan style because nothing done the traditional way, whether cooking or weaving or decorating a wall, happens quickly. Surfaces covered in tile mosaic, carved and painted wood, and carved plaster can take days or weeks to complete.

Sharing characterizes Moroccan living because this is not a culture for loners. People cook, bathe, play music, and practice age-old crafts together. In most Moroccan kitchens, you will find at least three women working together while they share news, gossip, and laughter. In the *souks,* groups of men and women work together weaving fabric, hammering bronze, and carving wood the way their ancestors did. Even bathing is a shared activity in a communal bathhouse called a *hammam,* where men and women visit on alternate days for long hours of scrubbing in steam baths heated by slow-burning wood fires.

Moroccan culture is so strong. It has evolved over more than two millennia and steadily integrated a wide range of foreign influences without ever losing its own uniquely regional identity. This evolution through integration has established the dual principles of tolerance and improvisation as the central spirit of the style—principles that are now guiding Moroccan style into the future. Fusion and diversity—words that only recently became common terms in the international dialogue about style and cuisine—form the very basis of this country's way of being.

Soon after that first trip to Morocco, my family decided to make Marrakech our holiday home, and ten years later we moved here full time. It was the perfect base for my new career as a hospitality and design entrepreneur as well as for my husband, Dr. Gary J. Martin's, work as an ethnobotanist and founder of the Global Diversity Foundation. In the ensuing years, I have witnessed a new vitality infusing the country in general and my city in particular. A vibrant energy is fueling the town as a new generation of Europeans and Americans arrives, restoring old houses and building new ones, opening restaurants, and starting design studios. I have recently met New Zealanders and Australians who are settling here, as well as Italians, Germans, and French.

These newcomers are creating a new Moroccan style by melding aspects of their native cultures and a contemporary design aesthetic with their own personal fantasies of Morocco. This style is a fresh celebration of the country's fascinating culture and its ability to blend, adapt, and evolve without weakening its identity. The new Moroccan style perpetuates the enduring concept of the Oriental fantasy—an exotic world characterized by beautiful architecture, extraordinary hospitality, and a sense of opulence and languor—while also offering an appealing and accessible approach to contemporary design and entertaining.

ABOVE: *The traditional Moroccan refreshment of mint tea and almond cookies is served in contemporary style on a terrace at Dar Tamsna, where furniture designed by Meryanne Loum-Martin reveals a fresh approach to familiar geometric designs.*

Perhaps this is why so many visitors are eager to bring home part of the lifestyle they encounter here and then create a Moroccan room in their house or a Moroccan terrace in their garden or throw Moroccan parties. By playing with rugs, candles, rose petals, spices, and cushions, it is possible to re-create the Moroccan dream anywhere. Even specific elements of Moroccan style are becoming easier to attain as importers around the world now stock pierced metal lamps, Moroccan carpets, *zellij*-topped tables, and *tagines*. Fortunately, lessons about combining unexpected colors, layering pattern and texture, and mixing for the most part familiar spices in unfamiliar ways can be absorbed after a visit to Morocco or even a few hours spent with this book. For this book not only celebrates the new Moroccan style I see unfolding around me but also encourages its continued flowering on Moroccan soil and beyond.

MERYANNE LOUM-MARTIN

OPPOSITE: *Bottles for per-fumes and fragrant oils are sensual accessories.*

BELOW: *In a tableau at Dar Tamsna, an art deco clock in front of a draw-ing of African wildlife expresses the fusion energy of North Africa.*

BELOW: *Meryanne often uses horns to inject an element of African wild-ness into her sophisti-cated furniture designs.*

Introduction ∽

MOROCCO'S RICH ARCHITECTURAL AND CULTURAL TRADITIONS, safeguarded in old walled cities, mountain villages, and oasis settlements, have fascinated Western visitors since the late nineteenth century. During the last decades of that century, French, English, and American artists and writers flocked to North Africa where they reveled in the mysterious beauty of its ancient towns and cities. They recorded what they saw in paintings and stories, familiarizing their compatriots with what they had admired. When they returned home, these travelers brought back carpets, colorful lanterns, and architectural fragments with which they created interiors inspired by the sensual spirit of the places they had visited.

These Orientalists, as they came to be known, helped spur a widespread fascination with Morocco and its decorative arts in late Victorian Europe and America, where it became all the rage to include Moroccan elements in domestic interiors and public places devoted to pleasure such as tearooms, shopping bazaars, beach pavilions, and a decade or two later, cinemas. This style, known as the Moorish revival, became synonymous with a decorative decadence celebrating exotic form, sensual texture, complex pattern, and traditional artisanship—all welcome elements in a Victorian world characterized by moral prudishness and the advent of industrially produced furnishings. As the burgeoning middle class sought a style to express their individuality (and members of the upper classes continued their ever constant quest for new and stylish modes of living), the Moorish revival flourished in Europe and America.

After several decades, however, the popularity of the Moroccan style waned as modernist movements eschewed excessive decoration in favor of pure geometry and unadorned functionalism. As lavish Moorish interiors received modernist makeovers, this once popular style nearly disappeared from sight. Only a few buildings in America and Europe remained to testify to its influence—and those were viewed as quaint reminders of turn-of-the-century eclecticism and excess.

RIGHT: *The Glaoui palace in Fez reveals many of the traditional elements of Andalusian ornamentation, including blue and white* zellij, *wet-carved plaster borders, and polychrome wood doors.*

OPPOSITE: *Expatriate American architect Stuart Church likes to vary the shapes of windows and doorways. Here he has created an opening in the shape of an Arabic perfume bottle for a garden pavilion built of handmade brick.*

18

Even as Western interest in the Moorish design idiom began to fade, the West's fascination with Morocco as a travel destination continued to grow. The government of the French Protectorate, formed in 1912, eased travel within the country, and the 1923 designation of Tangiers as an international free zone helped establish the beautiful city on the Strait of Gibraltar as a playground for the rich and famous. Celebrities, artists, and writers including Tennessee Williams, Paul Bowles, William Burroughs, Jack Kerouac, Marlene Dietrich, Elizabeth Taylor, and Tallulah Bankhead flocked to Tangiers in the 1920s, 1930s, 1940s, and 1950s.

Wealthy Europeans and Americans built second homes along the coast, and entrepreneurs constructed grand hotels that combined art deco and Moorish motifs and catered to the growing tourist population. While the writers and artists were, like their Orientalist predecessors, attracted to the evocative, timeless quality of Morocco's old quarters, the celebrities and partygoers came to participate in the seductive lifestyle they had come to associate with the country.

At the close of the twentieth century, a third wave of Morocco mania began, driven by a combination of continued fascination with the country as an exotic tourist destination and a revival of interest in its architecture and crafts. During the last few decades, King Hassan II and his son, King Mohammed VI, spearheaded several initiatives designed to protect and preserve Morocco's architectural heritage and to foster the continued practice of

its age-old crafts. They encouraged the purchase of architecturally significant palaces and private homes by Westerners with the financial resources to restore and transform these properties into guesthouses, hotels, and restaurants catering to a new generation of tourists.

Today, interior designers; architects; and textile, furniture, and ceramic artists from around the world are setting up shop in Morocco, creating homes for themselves, restoring old buildings and designing new villas for their fellow Westerners, and developing lines of decorative objects. While the Moorish revival of the late nineteenth century drew inspiration from Morocco in order to produce designs enjoyed in the West, this new revival is finding explosive expression and avid consumption right on Moroccan soil. Marrakech is the capital of the new Moroccan style, with its growing population of expatriate Europeans and Americans and booming tourist trade, but the movement is also gathering force in Fez, Essaouira, and Casablanca.

Outside of North Africa, the new Moroccan style is gaining the momentum of a major international design trend. The growing preoccupation with Moroccan style reflects an ennui with the cool mood of modernism and the predictable recycling of American and European decorative styles that have shaped the Western design world for the last fifty years. The growing interest in Moroccan style also reflects Morocco's position as an increasingly popular tourist destination among international travelers. Visitors from Europe and America continue to discover its temperate climate, exotic beauty, savory cuisine, and tradition-infused lifestyle. Like the paintings of nineteenth-century Orientalists, the photographs published in style and travel magazines reaching readers numbering in the millions are tantalizing Westerners with images of Morocco.

Once again, tourists return home with souvenirs from their travels and seek to re-create the luxurious interiors and gardens they encountered during their sojourns in Morocco. People who haven't even been there absorb ideas from magazines and books. They are designing Moroccan dining rooms, bedrooms, and baths; planting Moroccan style courtyard gardens; and hosting Moroccan parties in tents or on rose-petal-strewn dining tables. A lively export boom is under way as

OPPOSITE: *In the richly decorated courtyards of Marrakech's Riad Enija, wicker armchairs in tropical shades of pink and green adds a welcoming touch of informality while hinting at bygone days of colonial indolence.*

Moroccan lamps, mosaic tables, brass trays, and carpets are shipped to destinations around the world. Moroccan bazaars featuring the country's famous handicrafts are opening up in major cities everywhere and restaurants serving steaming *tagines*, couscous, and confections scented with orange-blossom water are burgeoning.

As the Moroccan style is once more being reinvented and repopularized within and beyond Morocco, a single enduring truth is becoming evident: the new Moroccan style is a fusion style that successfully marries a wide range of cultural influences, both Eastern and Western. Critics of the Orientalists and proponents of the late-nineteenth-century Moorish revival accused them of borrowing indiscriminately from a wide range of Islamic, North African, and Asian sources. But these critics overlooked the fact that Moroccan style has always been a hybrid aesthetic incorporating many centuries of influences from North Africa, Arabia, Persia, Syria, Turkey, Rome, Spain, France, and even China, indirectly. By boldly continuing this tradition on native soil, the creators of the new Moroccan style are demonstrating both the appropriateness and the rich potential of this fluid and eclectic approach to design.

THE ROOTS OF THE NEW MOROCCAN STYLE

The new Moroccan style stands on four cornerstones. The first of these is the architectural and decorative influence of the Berbers, African people who have lived in the deserts and mountains of Morocco since prehistoric times and whose descendants formed several powerful dynasties. Berber architecture includes the mysterious and menacing castles of red earth called *kasbahs* from which the lords of the Atlas controlled the passage of caravans from afar. Berber crafts include colorful carpets designed with bold stripes and geometric patterns and carved wooden doors incised with animistic motifs. The creators of the new Moroccan style find inspiration in the patterns, textures, colors, and shapes of ancient Berber designs as well as their traditional building materials, handmade bricks and rough wooden beams among them.

OPPOSITE: *Meryanne Loum-Martin designed a minimalist courtyard for her family's new palmeraie villa, fading color out to sunbleached ivory and simplifying typical Moroccan architectural elements including arches, carved cedar doors, and* mousharabiya.

23

The Arab armies that swept North Africa in the seventh century A.D. and established Islam as the region's dominant religious and cultural force laid the second cornerstone of the new Moroccan style. Along with a new religion and language, they also brought with them a new design vocabulary. Because traditional Islamic tenets forbid the representation of living beings, this new language consisted of elaborate patterns of stars and other geometric shapes, abstracted plant forms, and the sinuous lines of calligraphy. The Arabs also introduced a new palette based on the brilliant blue-and-white glazed tiles made by Persian craftsmen, who were in turn influenced by Chinese ceramics.

After conquering North Africa, the invading Arab army pressed on into Spain, where it established Islamic strongholds by the early eighth century. By doing so, it set in place the third cornerstone of the new Moroccan style: the Hispano-Muslim style, popularly known as Andalusian or Moorish. This style represented a marriage of Arab and Berber influences with the Hispano-Roman culture of southern Spain. For a period of several centuries ending with the Christian Reconquest in 1462 and the ultimate expulsion of Muslims and Jews from Spain in the early seventeenth century, Islamic and Jewish craftsmen traveled back and forth across the Strait of Gibraltar, refining this exotic hybrid of Middle Eastern and Mediterranean influence in their architecture, gardens, music, and cuisine.

The Andalusian style reached its zenith during the eleventh, twelfth, and thirteenth centuries, during which the Almoravid, Almohad, and Merinid dynasties built palaces, mosques, and universities in Spanish and Moroccan capitals of power. Of these, two major monuments remain to testify to the lavish beauty of Andalusian design: the Alhambra in Granada and the Quaraouiyine University in Fez. *Zellij*, the intricate geometric mosaics of cut ceramic tile that decorate floors, walls, columns, and fountains, and *tagguebbast*, filigree-like borders and panels of plaster carved while it is still damp into complex and delicate patterns, are two of the hallmarks of Andalusian design. This period also witnessed the refinement of an enduring architectural form of palaces and private houses constructed around courtyards, often filled with fragrant gardens and fountains, and surrounded by arcades and wrought-iron balconies.

The French set in place the final cornerstone of the new Moroccan style during the period of their protectorate, from 1912 to 1956. They brought with them the clean lines, bold geometries, and full volumes of the art deco style. Fortunately, the French also showed respect for the existing architecture they found in cities where they established communities. Rather than raze the old walled cities, they built modern ones outside the medina walls. They imported European building techniques and architects to construct buildings in the art deco style, often incorporating decorative flourishes borrowed from Morocco. With its pure geometric forms and strong colors, Andalusian decoration proved to be a perfect complement to the European art deco style, as demonstrated most famously at Marrakech's La Mamounia Hotel, which opened its doors to an international clientele in 1923.

ABOVE: *Over-the-top mirrors and pendant lights abound amid the glowing* tadlekt-*lined rooms of Yacout, the famous Marrakech restaurant designed by expatriate American Bill Willis.*

VISIONARIES OF THE NEW MOROCCAN STYLE

Meryanne Loum-Martin, one of the major proponents of the new Moroccan style, made her mark in the late 1980s by creating a resort just outside of Marrakech building upon all four of these cultural cornerstones. While most other hospitality entrepreneurs were recycling a typical array of Andalusian ingredients in predictable ways, Loum-Martin broadened her frame of reference while simplifying her shapes and unifying her palette to create a strong, new statement.

The villas at Dar Tamsna incorporate traditional Moroccan materials: glazed ceramic tile floors, walls of polished plaster (called *tadlekt*) punctuated with *zellij* and *tagguebbast* details, and decorative screens of turned wood and iron. But Loum-Martin integrated these familiar ingredients into a postmodern architectural

setting that blends subtle references to art deco and Hispano-Muslim design. For her color scheme, Loum-Martin, a Frenchwoman of Senegalese descent, drew on her associations of Africa as a place of sun-burnished earth tones. For furnishings, she created new designs for chairs, tables, beds, and lamps that merged Berber, Moorish, and art deco influences in an unfussy fusion style. This resort captured the imagination of the European jet set, who book weeklong stays and fashion shoots there years in advance, as well as the interest of the international media, which feature Dar Tamsna in books, magazines, and style programs broadcast around the world.

Loum-Martin serves as a link between the first wave of modern Moroccan design initiated in the late 1970s and early 1980s by the visionary designer Bill Willis and architectural genius Charles Boccara and the new generation of designers and architects working in Morocco today. Willis, an expatriate American who studied at Columbia University and Cooper Union in New York and the École des Beaux-Arts in Paris before settling in Marrakech in the 1970s, chose the forms, surface decoration, and typical furnishings of the Andalusian Golden Age as his medium.

Willis looked at these with the fresh eyes of an American designer, recognizing their value as pure design elements. He began to apply *zellij* in eye-popping patterns and found new uses for *tadlekt*, the water-resistant polished plaster previously relegated to the walls of the traditional steam bath, or *hammam*. Willis brought *tadlekt* out of the dimly lit bathrooms and into living rooms, hallways, and spiraling staircases where its gleaming, variegated surface dazzled the eye. He also employed a technique called *grattage*, in which alternating bands of *tadlekt* are polished and sanded, to create delightfully unexpected surfaces and patterns.

OPPOSITE: *At Caravan-Serai, Mathieu Boccara reveals the influence of his father, architect Charles Boccara.*

ABOVE: *Charles Boccara's home outside Marrakech demonstrates his passion for monumental scale.*

27

Willis also brought a whimsical spirit to the houses he designed for such clients as Yves Saint Laurent, Paul Getty, and the Rothschilds, as well as his most widely visited creation, the dining rooms and terraces of Marrakech's Yacout restaurant. In these decors, he employed *zellij; tadlekt;* and playfully opulent lanterns, mirrors, and furnishings of his own design to create hypnotically hedonistic settings. By doing so, he introduced an element of delirium and free-wheeling fantasy that has continued to intoxicate and inspire.

While Willis redefined the Moroccan interior, Charles Boccara reinvigorated the country's architecture with his robust designs in which he combines the primal presence of *kasbahs* and *ksour* (fortified Berber villages) with the majesty of classical monuments. This Tunisian-born, Paris-trained architect has designed several of Marrakech's most distinctive hotels and resorts and recently completed what will likely be his most enduring legacy, a monumental opera house in Marrakech. Boccara's designs range from the modern Moorish art deco style Tichka Hotel to the Deux Tours resort and Marrakech Opera House where Moroccan, Egyptian, Roman, and Turkish influences all blend in an architecture that invokes the mystery and nobility of ancient ruins.

While employing many of the materials and forms associated with the Hispano-Muslim style, Boccara also delves deeply and widely into the roots of Moroccan and African style. He reintroduced ancient Berber building materials including *pisé* (pounded red earth reinforced with straw) and mud bricks, and he borrowed such architectural forms as lotus-shaped columns from Egypt and the vaulted arches and soaring domes of Rome and Byzantium. Boccara combines these elements in buildings characterized by a dignity that is simultaneously earthy and intellectual. By doing so, he liberates these materials and forms from the bounds of tradition and demonstrates their relevance to contemporary design. He also inspired a new generation of architects and designers in Morocco including his former protégé, architect Elie Mouyal, and his own son, Mathieu Boccara, who recently opened a resort called CaravanSerai that pays overt homage to his father's influence.

LEFT: *A refined Orientalism reigns in the serene rooms of Riyad El Mezouar where nineteenth-century paintings of Turkish sultans share space with contemporary design.*

By borrowing freely from the past and integrating their discoveries in free-wheeling design statements, Willis and Boccara set in motion the design revolution that is now flowering in Morocco and beyond. Today, architects and designers feel free to plunder the inexhaustible treasure trove of Morocco's design traditions and employ their selections in highly individual creations that reflect the full range of contemporary taste.

RIGHT: *To achieve an air of elegant repose at Riyad El Mezouar, designers Jérôme Vermelin and Michel Durand-Meyrier replaced cheaply made* zellij *tiles with plaster and stripped carved doors back to their original wood.*

In the new Moroccan style, FUSION has expanded to include not only North African, Mediterranean, and French colonial influences but also Indian, contemporary Italian, and Swedish design. A new MINIMALISM, once unthinkable in Morocco's more-is-better approach to decor, is gaining ground as designers discover ways to tone down the polychrome palette and busy ornamentation associated with Moroccan style. DELIRIUM, a mood swinging from dreamy reverie to fevered trances, has never gone out of style in Morocco, and today's architects and designers are growing ever more imaginative in their efforts to enthrall and enchant. Meanwhile, hoteliers, architects, and interior designers are also exploring the mood of REPOSE, that state of grace invoked by quiet cloisters, fragrant gardens, and serene surroundings.

In the following pages, you will meet the visionaries who are forging this new Moroccan style in Morocco and beyond, in private homes, intimate guesthouses and resorts, and stylish restaurants and hotels. You will step inside their private worlds and discover the materials, techniques, and aesthetics they employ to create unforgettable experiences of fusion, minimalism, delirium, and repose. Then you may follow their example by delving into this treasure chest of ideas and images to create your own personal interpretation of Moroccan style. Welcome to the sensual and surprising world of the new Moroccan style.

BELOW: *A nineteenth-century bowl from Fez is filled with silver beads from Sana'a in Yemen.*

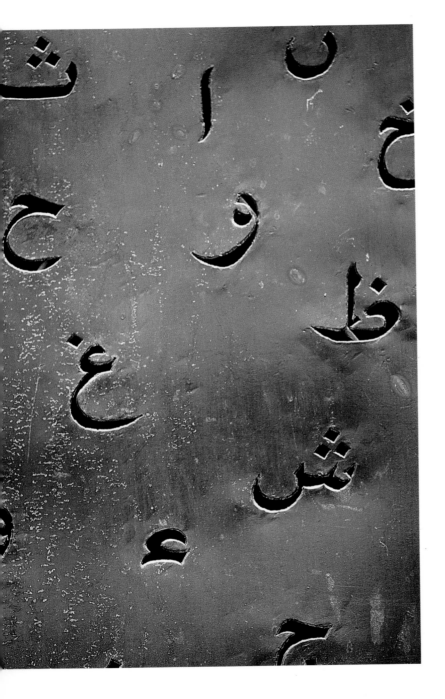

Elements of the New Moroccan Style

A growing community of designers from around the world are living in Morocco, where they are creating new decorative objects for an increasingly style-hungry, trend-savvy audience. These furnishings, textiles, tableware, and other objects offer contemporary interpretations of traditional Moroccan patterns, textures, silhouettes, and materials. While these designers draw inspiration from Morocco's ancient history of craftsmanship, they are also interjecting an increasingly global set of influences: hot Madras colors, cool Italian silhouettes, American playfulness, Parisian restraint.

While many of the new designers have set up shop in the newer quarters of Morocco's cities—the modern boulevards that lie beyond the walls of the old medinas—there is also a large population of craftspeople living within the *souks* who are fashioning wood, ceramic, metal, and fiber objects in exactly the same way their ancestors have been doing for centuries. Together, these designers and craftspeople provide the building blocks of the new Moroccan style—a dynamic marriage of the antique and the contemporary, the rustic and the refined, the familiar and the utterly unexpected.

OPPOSITE: *Calligraphic renderings of Arab text have long been an element of traditional Andalusian design. The pierced metal door at Riad 72 in Marrakech translates this tradition into a contemporary minimalist expression.*

RIGHT: *At Yacout, Bill Willis used the conventional material of blue and white* zellij *to create eye-popping Op effects.*

LEFT: *Bed linens designed by Taoufiq Baroudi offer a simplified approach to Morocco's typically complex geometric patterns.*

33

LEFT: Tadlekt, *a variegated surface made by polishing and waxing plaster to which dry pigment has been added, can be created in any imaginable color, from this cool green to rich red and glossy aubergine.*

OPPOSITE: *At Dar Noor Charana, a guesthouse in Marrakech, Elisabeth Dianda sets her table with linens and ceramics hand-embellished with the geometric patterns favored by Berber artisans.*

LEFT: *Straw prayer mats woven with red bands of pattern are ubiquitous in Morocco. At Riyad el Cadi, they are attached to a wall, where they add texture as well as color.*

BELOW: *Woven branches of pliable wood such as oleander are used to create decorative ceilings, whether left in their natural state, as here, or painted in bright colors.*

OPPOSITE: *Doors of cedar and other durable woods carved with elaborate geometric designs are common features in Moroccan homes. This gate from the home of Charles Boccara features a mesmerizing design of interconnected spirals.*

RIGHT: *For the minimalist-style guesthouse Dar Kawa, designer Charlotte Barkowski created a line of ceramics that marries modernist restraint with the primitive purity of Cycladic figurines.*

LEFT: *Meals at the Tamsna resorts are served on the Tamsna pattern of china inspired by Moroccan decorative motifs, created by designer Arielle de Brichambaut, and manufactured by Limoges.*

OPPOSITE: *In another line of sophisticated tableware featured at several of Marrakech's minimalist-style riads, Charlotte Barkowski uses high-gloss glazes in rich shades of gray.*

LEFT: *A silk shawl by Paige Hathaway Thorn is screened with calligraphy; slippers, by Meryanne Loum-Martin, are inspired by traditional Moroccan styles.*

LEFT: *A canopy made from Carolyn Quartermaine silk adds a contemporary note to this traditional Andalusian-style bedroom at Riad Enija.*

BELOW: *Sumptuous silk pillows in burnished earth tones by designer Taoufiq Baroudi perch atop a secretary by Michel Durand-Meyrier and Jérôme Vermelin.*

41

ABOVE: *The textures and patinas of a braided straw chair, a nubby Berber carpet, a rough-hewn table, and a hand-thrown ceramic bowl evoke the rugged quality of rustic Berber design.*

BELOW: *Working in the distinctly non-Moroccan material of cast, cut, and welded steel, former sculptor Frederic Butz creates sleek contemporary furniture that evokes the sweeping geometries of Moroccan architecture.*

LEFT: *This chest of drawers inset with* tadlekt *panels is the work of expatriate Italian designer Luciano Monti, who creates furniture in contemporary styles using the traditional materials and methods of Moroccan artisans.*

fusion

LOCATED ON THE NORTHWESTERN CORNER OF AFRICA,
Morocco faces two seas, the Atlantic and the Mediterranean, and nearly touches Spain across the Strait of Gibraltar. Over a period of more than two thousand years, Greek, Roman, Byzantine, Spanish, Portuguese, English, German, and French visitors have crossed these waters to reach Morocco. And armies of Arabian and Moorish invaders have traveled the opposite way, carrying their religion, architecture, music, and cuisine across the water to El Andalus, as southern Spain was once called.

African Berbers living in camel hair tents and *pisé kasbahs*, Moorish potentates feasting in *zellij*-covered courtyards, and French colonialists enjoying cocktails in swank art deco hotels have all called Morocco home. Each generation has left its mark on this country where fusion is the very essence of design and cuisine. The Andalusian style, the refined decorative architecture of the Hispano-Moorish era, is considered by many to be the purest expression of Moroccan style, but it is, in fact, a hybrid of Middle Eastern and Mediterranean elements. Many of the ingredients and preparations that are associated with Moroccan cuisine also trace their origins to countries lying to the east and west of Morocco's borders.

By the late nineteenth century in Europe, Moorish revival architects and Orientalist artists freely mingled aspects of Andalusian style with Indian, Chinese, and Turkish fantasies. Back on Moroccan soil, the French colonialists added their own ideas, effortlessly blending the stylized patterns and geometric shapes of art deco with the country's existing designs. Today, a whole new generation of North Africans, Europeans, and Americans is once more redefining fusion in Morocco and beyond. Whether preserving an art deco-infused family home, updating exotic Orientalist fantasies, or forging a sophisticated twenty-first-century global aesthetic, these homeowners, hoteliers, and restaurateurs are demonstrating the infinite adaptability of Moroccan style.

Refashioning Fusion

DAR TAMSNA

In the late 1980s, Meryanne Loum-Martin's family purchased a walled compound in the *palmeraie* outside of Marrakech where two unfinished buildings stood amid a grove of date palm trees and overgrown lantana. Today, these two structures, transformed into fashionable villas surrounded by green lawns and lavishly blooming gardens, are some of the *palmeraie*'s most sought after resort properties. At Dar Tamsna, Loum-Martin created a new look for Moroccan style by finding a perfect balance between the boldly masculine proportions of art deco design, the earthy textures and colors of *kasbahs,* and the unabashedly romantic patterns of Andalusian design. Loum-Martin brought a refined European sensibility that reflected her years of living in Paris. She also injected two elements not previously found in the fusion vocabulary of the new Moroccan style: hand-woven Senegalese textiles and clean-edged contemporary furniture she designed herself. "I love the highly decorated quality of the Moroccan and Syrian furniture that you see so much of here," Meryanne explains, "but it needs to be balanced by something

46

LEFT AND OPPOSITE:
Traditional elements of Moroccan decor found at Dar Tamsna include mother-of-pearl inlaid pieces from Syria, intricately carved wooden chairs and tables, large bronze trays, and colorful Turkish kilim carpets. To these, Meryanne adds more contemporary elements, including art deco-inspired torchières, oversized bronze urns and vases, and furniture of her own design fashioned from burnished metal and wood.

LEFT: *For al fresco meals, crisp white table linens and chair covers provide refined contrast to the earth-colored architectural setting. Plentiful white candles and torches provide flickering light and the surrounding garden scents the air.*

BELOW: *Patterns of zellij decorate outdoor nooks where guests can relax in dappled sunlight.*

50

much simpler and more severe." To fill this need, she drew up designs for iron chaise longues, cedar chairs, and upholstered divans that merged geometric silhouettes with abstracted motifs borrowed from indigenous African designs.

Meryanne's departure from the typical Andalusian-based style of Morocco, with its color schemes of white, blue, green, and yellow, was to adopt a palette of bronzed reds and sun-burned browns, of sand-colored beige and earth brick. Using these colors, she decorated sensual salons and dining rooms in the two villas, Nakhil and Ouardaia, and an intimate cottage.

In Nakhil, the floors of the living rooms are covered with "Moroccan marble," a richly variegated stone from Ifrane. In the Ouardaia salon, she created walls of deep rose *tadlekt* accented by more intensely colored details including canopies made by hanging red Turkish rugs from the ceiling.

Traditional materials such as carved plaster cornices and cedar ceilings spark Moroccan fantasies, while roughly woven textiles from Senegal, candelabra made from water buffalo horns, and drawings of elephants and tigers invoke a larger African context. Jazz Age details—a rhythmically zigzagging canopy enclosing a divan and period art deco chairs—provide reminders of the French colonial overlay of Western style that infiltrated many parts of Africa in the early twentieth century.

In the villas' bedrooms, Meryanne explores a cooler range of color, bringing in the soft greens and vibrant yellows of the garden. One bedroom, all white on white, offers the perfect antidote to Morocco's color-drenched environment. Another, a green retreat with a bed draped in a simple canopy of cotton canvas, offers cool sanctuary. But some of the best retreats of all can be found outside, in shady verandas comfortably furnished with large divans and garden nooks hidden among the bougainvillea, lantana, and rosebushes.

At Dar Tamsna, Meryanne also forged a new style of entertaining that, like the decor, blends European refinement (white linens and Limoges), Moroccan ingredients (spiced olives and fluffy couscous), and modernist restraint (no belly dancers or riotous colors on the table or the plate). Most meals at Dar Tamsna are served outside, despite the fact that the compound's two villas both have handsome

LEFT: *Morocco's African, Arabic, Andalusian, and French colonial identities merge harmoniously in this contemporary living room. The fireplace combines the Arab-Andalusian element of wet-carved plaster (executed in a contemporary pattern) within an art deco-inspired frame of setback rectangles. Textiles from Senegal dress furniture designed by Meryanne and inspired by traditional Moroccan styles.*

dining rooms. Morning coffee and tea are sipped in semi-enclosed terraces overlooking lawns, pools, and the snow-topped peaks of the Atlas Mountains. Cocktails are served beneath the stars on verandas, porches, and roof terraces.

In the evening, formal dinners are set on tables placed on the lawn. With the natural beauty of the garden setting and the villas' dramatic facades, there is no need for ornate table decorations. Loum-Martin dresses her tables simply with heavy white linens, freshly cut blooms, and white candles arranged in oversized lanterns and candelabra. For china, she commissioned a friend, designer Arielle de Brichambaut, to create an elegant pattern called Dar Tamsna (manufactured by Limoges) that features Moroccan motifs.

These elegant table settings demonstrate that in Morocco neither decor nor hospitality need be elaborate, excessive, and overstimulating. In addition to widening the vocabulary of Moroccan style, Meryanne also succeeded in lowering the volume, reminding people that simple elegance is equally—and perhaps even more—expressive of true Moroccan style than opulent excess.

LEFT: *Deep blue and pale green enameled tiles provide cool visual and textural relief in a fountain that splashes gently throughout the day in Dar Tamsna's garden.*

OPPOSITE: *Dramatically sweeping staircases lie at the heart of the Dar Tamsna villas, inviting guests to climb to rooftop terraces from which they can survey the sky.*

54

Sensual History

DINNER AT LA MAISON BLEUE

A sequence of heavy wooden doors and dimly lit passages lead to the heart of La Maison Bleue. The first of these doors opens off a busy street that gradually winds its way into the labyrinth of the Fez medina. But travelers need not venture far down this road to experience the ancient city's charm. By turning in to the entrance of La Maison Bleue and traveling through its rosewater-scented halls, they quickly fall beneath Fez's exotic spell. ✺ Thanks to its centuries-old interaction with Spain, Fez is in many ways the mother of Andalusian style. The style finds nearly pure expression at La Maison Bleue, a family palace built circa 1915 by Mohammed El Abbadi, a renowned judge and astrologer of the time. "At La Maison Bleue, you are first and foremost the guests of a prominent Fassi family in their own home," explains Mehdi El Abbadi, who with his sister Kenza manages the property as a guesthouse and restaurant. ✺ The architecture of the palace illustrates the hallmarks of Andalusian design. Blue-and-white *zellij* covers the lower portions of the walls in

OPPOSITE: *Though less than 100 years old, La Maison Bleue has the hallmarks of the much older Andalusian style: intricately detailed wood and plaster carvings,* zellij, *and ornamental wrought iron. The mixture of traditional Moroccan furnishings with European antiques and art deco designs is typical of stylish Fez homes of the early twentieth century.*

ABOVE: *Formal European furniture adds another level of decadence to the already opulent atrium at La Maison Bleue.*

the atrium, and a *zellij* pattern of yellow flowers on blue ribbons spreads like carefully arranged garlands across the floor. Tall doors fashioned from cedar and carved with patterns of radiating stars hang from ornamental hinges shaped like miniature parapets. Intricate designs of carved plaster cascade like frozen waterfalls from the upper reaches of the walls. The sound of water echoes through the tall chamber, glancing off the walls of a tile-lined niche where a fountain flows throughout the day and night. The three other walls of the atrium open into *salons marocains,* long rooms lined with banquettes upholstered in brocade and heaped with cushions.

While these details can be found in Moroccan palaces several centuries older than La Maison Bleue, other decorative elements reveal the twentieth-century nature of this particular home. "Our family has lived in this house for three generations," explains Kenza. "The decorations are all original and reflect the taste of an old Fassi family." These furnishings demonstrate the worldly fusion that occurred in sophisticated Moroccan homes during the early twentieth century. Venetian glass chandeliers and mirrors with petal-like layers of glass hang in the salons. Ornate Italian brocade and handmade lace drape the arched doorways; streamlined art deco sconces illuminate the walls. The furniture in the atrium includes art deco and Louis XV chairs, low coffee tables fashioned from screens of turned wood called *mousharabiya,* and English silver candelabra.

Unlike visiting a museum where the past is carefully quarantined from the present, the experience of spending the night or enjoying a meal at La Maison Bleue is a direct and sensual dose of living history. During dinner candelabra bristle with tapers that lend a flickering light to the cavernous atrium. Musicians strum lutes and sing Andalusian ballads with meandering medieval melodies while servers in colorful tunics deliver cocktails and bowls of green olives laced with spices.

When dinner is ready, guests proceed to the salons where cloths decorated with cross-stitch patterns of *point de Fez* embroidery cover the tables. Flat rounds of bread are passed while the server brings seven small earthenware *tagines* filled with lightly dressed vegetable salads that tempt diners to eat far more than they should during this first of many courses. When the waiter returns with a steaming platter, the salon fills with an herbal fragrance, and Kenza explains the origins of the dish—a chicken in green sauce often savored by the Abbadi family on special occasions.

Each night of the week, a different meat course is served, followed by either pigeon pie—a savory Fez specialty—or a platter of couscous. "Couscous of the Thirteenth Century," the waiter proudly announces this night as he delivers a conical mound of the lightest semolina decorated with a geometric pattern of crushed almonds and cinnamon. Tender pieces of stewed beef are tucked into the mound and a tiny saucer of powdered sugar is passed around, its sweetness adding another dimension to the dish.

At the end of dinner at La Maison Bleue, it seems impossible to summon any appetite for dessert, but when the waiter returns with a plate crowned by a layered confection of pastry and custard, it is impossible to turn him away. This last dish—Pastilla with Milk Custard—is accompanied by sliced oranges sprinkled with cinnamon and orange flower water. Distilled from the blossoms of Seville orange trees, this elixir whispers reminders of the lush gardens of the Alhambra—the ancient Andalusian seat of Islam. As if on cue, the musicians begin to strum medieval melodies that echo the exotic flavors of the meal and complete the sensual history lesson taught so deliciously at La Maison Bleue.

BELOW: *At Riad Maison Bleue, guests enjoy breakfast served in a shaded loggia overlooking the swimming pool.*

Menu

Seven Moroccan Salads
(including Beets in
Lemon and Parsley Vinaigrette
and a Salad of Green
Peppers and Tomatoes)*

Chicken in a Green Herb Sauce

Couscous of the Thirteenth Century

Pastilla with Milk Custard

*recipes not included

Chicken in a Green Herb Sauce
(Serves 4)

1 chicken (about 3 pounds), cut into serving pieces
2 tablespoons olive oil
2 tablespoons vegetable oil
1 peeled piece fresh ginger (about 2 inches)
$^{1}/_{2}$ cup water
4 garlic cloves, finely chopped
$^{1}/_{4}$ teaspoon saffron threads, toasted and crushed
1 large bunch parsley, chopped

Pastilla with Milk Custard

1 large bunch cilantro, chopped
Salt and freshly ground black pepper to taste

Sprinkle the chicken pieces with salt and pepper. Heat both oils in a large, deep skillet over medium-high heat. When the oil is hot, brown the chicken. Remove the chicken to a clean bowl and reserve the oil in the pan.

Slice the ginger into rounds and put them in a blender with the water. Puree until a paste forms. Reduce the heat under the pan where the chicken was cooked to medium and place the garlic in the oil, sautéing for 1 minute. Add the saffron and cook for 1 minute. Add the ginger paste and cook for 3 minutes. Add the chicken pieces along with any juices from the bowl. Cover and cook over medium-low heat, turning the chicken occasionally, for 25 minutes. Season with salt and pepper. Add the parsley and cilantro, stirring to mix with the juices in the pan. Cook, covered, for 5 more minutes, or until the chicken is cooked through.

Couscous of the Thirteenth Century
(Serves 4)

Note: If you are serving this dish as an entrée, you may wish to double the amount of meat to 1 pound.

4 tablespoons olive oil
$^{1}/_{2}$ pound lean, tender cut of beef or lamb,

Add the onions to the pan and season with salt and pepper. Cook over medium heat until golden and soft but not browned. Return the meat to the pan and add the water. Cook, covered, over medium heat for one hour or until the meat is very tender. Remove the meat from the pan. Strain the sauce through a sieve to remove whole spices and onions, reserving the sauce.

Spread one half of the hot couscous in a flat layer on a large serving platter. Place the meat and $1/2$ cup of the pan juices in the center of the layer. Mound the remaining couscous over the first layer to create a conical shape. Place the crushed almonds into a plastic bag and snip a corner open. Release the almonds in neat intersecting lines across the top of the couscous. Take large pinches of cinnamon and draw more intersecting lines across the couscous. Serve while hot with a small bowl of confectioners' sugar that can be passed as a garnish.

cut into bite-sized pieces

2 cinnamon sticks

10 saffron threads, toasted and crushed

2 medium onions, sliced

Salt and freshly ground black pepper to taste

$1/2$ cup water

4 cups cooked couscous

$1/2$ cup almonds, toasted and finely crushed

2 tablespoons ground cinnamon

Confectioners' sugar for garnish

Heat the oil in a large, deep skillet over medium-high heat. Brown the meat. Remove it from the heat and reserve. Reduce the heat to medium. Add the cinnamon sticks and saffron to the pan and cook for 1 minute.

Pastilla with Milk Custard
(Serves 4)

Note: This pastry dish is traditionally made with *warqa*, a thin dough similar to phyllo. Because this is difficult to purchase outside of Morocco, phyllo is substituted in this recipe.

2 large eggs

$4^{1}/_{4}$ cups whole milk

½ cup sugar

4 teaspoons cornstarch

2 teaspoons orange flower water

1 package 14 × 18-inch sheets phyllo dough, thawed

½ cup unsalted butter, melted

⅓ cup almonds, toasted and crushed

Preheat the oven to 350 degrees F. In a large bowl, beat the eggs until whites and yolks are well mixed. Then add 4 cups of the milk and the sugar. Dissolve the cornstarch in the remaining ¼ cup of milk. Add this to the milk-and-egg mixture and stir. Pour the custard into a large, heavy-bottomed saucepan and bring to a simmer over medium-low heat. Cook, stirring frequently, for about 30 minutes or until the custard is thick enough to coat the back of a spoon. Do not allow the custard to boil. Stir in the orange flower water. Refrigerate until cold.

Prepare a stack of 3 sheets of phyllo dough, laying 1 sheet on top of the other and brushing each with melted butter (keep remaining pastry sheets covered with a damp towel or plastic wrap). Place a 12-inch-diameter plate on top of the pastry, and using a sharp knife, cut around the edge of the plate to create a circle of dough. Place the phyllo, buttered side down, on a cookie sheet. Brush butter on top of the circle of dough. Repeat these steps three times to create 4 disks of phyllo.

Bake the disks for 12 to 15 minutes or until golden and crisp. Cool on a wire rack. Then stack with paper towels in between each disk until ready to assemble the dish.

Mint tea and sweets at Riad Maison Bleue

On a large serving platter, place 1 disk of baked phyllo and cover with a quarter of the custard. Keep stacking layers of phyllo and custard until all the phyllo disks and custard have been used, finishing with a layer of custard. Sprinkle the top of the disk with crushed almonds and serve immediately by bringing to the table whole and cutting into wedges.

A Connoisseur's Retreat

RIYAD EL CADI

OPPOSITE: *Antique doors of polychrome wood add color and pattern to Bartels's modernist interpretation of Moroccan style.*

P eople decorating interiors in Morocco for use by Western tourists often tend to create burlesque interpretations of the nation's style. With little discrimination or individuality, they throw together busy *zellij,* colorful *tadlekt,* elaborately turned *mousharabiya,* brightly painted doors and ceilings, Berber rugs, and pierced metal lamps. When they are done, they shout, "*Voilà!* Moroccan style!" This lamentable approach to decor, which results in overdecorated, underpersonalized interiors, is something that Ambassador Herwig Bartels made every effort to avoid when restoring and decorating the fourteenth-century structure he purchased in Marrakech's old Berber quarter. ᴏ—ᴡ The German ambassador to Morocco for five years, a lifetime diplomat whose work has taken him to Cairo, Beirut, Damascus, and Amman, and a collector, Bartels is a connoisseur of design in the Arab world. As such, he has a fine appreciation for the complexity and subtlety of Morocco's decorative tradition. But Bartels is also a modernist with a passion for the clean lines and spare elegance of

65

RIGHT: *Centuries-old tiles found during the restoration process decorate the dining room's fireplace. A table combining contemporary iron and antique wood from Borneo and a seventeenth-century Anatolian kilim demonstrate the ease with which Bartels combines objects from the past and present.*

66

LEFT: *Bartels replaced cheaply made blue and white tile in the main courtyard with sand-colored tiles with green highlights. The sixteenth-century fountain's zellij panel is a modern inter-pretation of a traditional Islamic pattern.*

BELOW: *A seventeenth-century Ottomon em-broidery and a late fifteenth-century Anatolian carpet fragment hang upon the walls; con-temporary fabric from Egyptian designer Fouad Sadek creates a diapha-nous shield from the hot sun.*

contemporary design. At his home and guesthouse, Riyad El Cadi, he successfully marries these two traits to forge an eclectic style that is unique and deeply personal.

Riyad El Cadi comprises several interconnected *riads,* or courtyard dwellings, that include twelve bedrooms, five courtyards, a large salon, a dining room, several rooftop terraces, and an art gallery. Over a period of several centuries, these *riads* had been separated into individual homes and many of the original architectural details had been replaced or covered over. With the assistance of Belgian architect Quentin Wilbaux, Bartels restored much of the structure to its original appearance, reopening old doorways and discovering ancient details including glazed tiles dating from the thirteenth or fourteenth century. In keeping with his modernist aesthetic, Bartels interpreted the ancient structure as simply as possible, respecting the basic materials of stucco, wood, and tile and avoiding displays of bright color and overwrought pattern.

Where Bartels has employed traditional Moroccan decorative elements, they never appear trite or gratuitous. Instead, they assume freshness in contrast to their restrained surroundings. For example, a fountain nestled into the walls of the central courtyard features only a small central plaque of *zellij:* a simplified interpretation of a traditional geometric design. For the colors of the tiles, Bartels found inspiration from sources as diverse as dark green enameled metal picnic plates given to him by

his daughter and the pale green glaze on ancient Chinese ceramics.

Bartels used this same celadon shade in the glazed tiles that form the courtyard floor where they alternate in a subtle pattern with sand-colored tiles. "When I bought the house, this courtyard was entirely covered with blue-and-white tiles that gave it such a cold look," Bartels recalls. "I retired to Morocco because I loved its warmth, its luminosity—and I wanted to capture that essence in my home." Warmth and luminosity are indeed constants throughout the house, whether provided in an open-air hallway by lengths of gauzy fabric that billow in the breeze or antique Berber textiles that hang on the walls as works of art.

In his collection of antiquities from within and beyond the Islamic world, Bartels favors objects that reveal a deep appreciation of color and the highest artisanal skills. A long brocaded carpet from nineteenth-century Turkey hanging in the dining room is one of the ambassador's favorite possessions. "It has a very rigid ground pattern and many different colors that blend perfectly into a textile of great beauty," he remarks. "In a way, it represents my own way of decorating—I have to establish a ground pattern, which for me is color, and as long as I respect the ground pattern, I am permitted to vary the other elements."

This approach to decorating is evident throughout Riyad El Cadi, particularly in the large living room where blood-red accents punctuate a monochromatic palette of white and beige. Bartels's inspiration for the color scheme came from a piece of Syrian Byzantine mosaic, now mounted in the room, that dates from the fourth or fifth century. An eclectic array of contemporary Western furniture and Asian pieces, including Ming dynasty armchairs, furnishes the room. "Good Chinese furniture done in the classical style tends to be so sober, so modern to our eyes, that it marries well with everything around it," Bartels observes.

70

A second-floor bedroom suite also demonstrates his skill at combining elements from diverse cultures. This room draws its palette from a large northern Moroccan fragment of antique paneling painted red and black. A kilim unfurled across the floor beneath it reflects these hues. A carving from a longhouse in Borneo bears the emblem of a dragon and hangs above a bed dressed with a traditional Berber wool coverlet finished with giant white pom-poms. This last detail hints at the sly sense of humor evident throughout the house that prevents the rarefied setting from over-awing guests.

In the kitchen, for example, a French art deco window inspired by Islamic design crowns a built-in cabinet. Industrial lighting hangs from the ceiling and a checkerboard pattern of black-and-white tile covers the floor. French copper molds are displayed on one wall and bright red Panton chairs of molded plastic, circa 1970, inject a lighthearted note. "I love the way you can combine antiquities with contemporary furniture," Bartels exclaims. By interweaving his fascination for antiquity with a love of modernism and blending his personal preferences with an informed appreciation of regional design, Bartels has created a unique interpretation of Moroccan style that celebrates the country's age-old spirit of fusion.

RIGHT: *An eleventh-century Byzantine cross, an earthenware pot from southern Morocco, and an Anatolian prayer kilim reveal the complex cultural polyrhythms of Bartels's collection of antiquities.*

An Orientalist Fete

COCKTAILS AT COMPTOIR DARNA

European artists flocked to North Africa in the last decades of the nineteenth century. Once there, these artists created paintings of the images they encountered, embellishing them with details that mingled real life with vivid fantasy about Oriental splendor and sensuality. Comptoir Darna, a French-owned restaurant and nightclub in Marrakech, capitalizes on the enduring allure of this Orientalist mode. ⌒～⌣ The brainchild of Marcel Chiche, who launched a Moroccan bar-restaurant in Paris called Comptoir Paris in the 1980s, Comptoir Darna was inspired by the success of this venture and the growing popularity of Marrakech as a destination for European tourists. When Comptoir Darna opened, there were already several high-end restaurants in Marrakech catering to the decadent fantasies of visiting Westerners who expect lavish multicourse feasts punctuated by the undulations of belly dancers. But Chiche succeeded in translating this clichéd Orientalist dream into a contemporary aesthetic that permeates the decor, menu, and entertainment at Comptoir.

OPPOSITE: *Smoky gray and smoldering red* tadlekt *creates a sultry mood at Le Comptoir.*

OVERLEAF: *A tapas-like menu of appetizers with a range of Mediterranean influences invites diners to enjoy long cocktail hours on the terrace, where low divans offer comfortable places to loll.*

BELOW: *Snails, a dish popular in both France and Morocco, are poached in a broth scented with cinnamon, fennel seed, and cloves.*

The highly charged, theatrical architecture blends traditional Moroccan elements (*tadlekt* surfaces and pierced metal lamps spangling the walls and ceiling with light) with Chinese details including a lacquer-red door and a Buddhist altar table. When guests pass through the vermilion door, they find themselves at the base of a sweeping staircase in the center of a cavernous room decorated in the colors of smoke and fire. Low tables and chairs invite diners to loll while picking at olives and sipping a house cocktail called the Sexy Drink.

The temperate Marrakech climate makes the cushion-strewn patio a favorite place to enjoy cocktails and hors d'oeuvres. This enclosed garden must serve as inspiration for anyone who has dreamed of creating an Oriental pleasure garden back home where they might amuse and amaze their friends with exotic food and drink. Low benches covered with orange, pink, and purple pillows cluster in the corners of the patio beneath a bower of tropical plants. Leather hassocks and tables of hammered copper and brass hold an inviting array of small plates filled with what Chiche describes as "Moroccan tapas."

An enthusiast of French, Moroccan, Japanese, and Mediterranean cuisines, Chiche has created a menu that mixes ingredients and ideas from each of these regions to surprising and satisfying effect. Escargots, a favorite of both French and Marrakechi diners, are poached in a spice-infused stock. Slices of marinated fish nestle on a bed of fried vermicelli with a side of Middle Eastern–inspired eggplant caviar. A Mediterranean style tapenade with a Moroccan twist combines black olives with almonds and basil.

The rewards of Comptoir belong to the adventurous who join in the spirit of innovation and enchantment Chiche invokes. Whether playing with food and drink, music (a constantly changing sound track blending house music with Andalusian and African strains), or mood (ranging from the cool hipsterism of the early-evening bar to the sizzling late-night floor show), Chiche creates a mesmerizing Orientalist fete for all who pass through Comptoir's doors.

The Sexy Drink
(Makes 1 drink)

1 peeled piece fresh ginger, about 4 inches
1/4 cup water
1/2 ounce simple syrup
1 1/2 ounces tequila

Slice the ginger into rounds and put them in a blender. Add the water and liquefy. Strain the mixture through a medium sieve and discard the solids. Combine 1/2 ounce of ginger juice with the simple syrup and tequila in a cocktail shaker and add crushed ice. Shake and serve straight up in a chilled martini glass or over ice. For a nonalcoholic beverage, substitute fresh orange juice for the tequila.

Basil-Olive Tapenade
(Makes 1¹/₂ cups)

Serve this savory spread with pita chips made by cutting pita into wedges and dividing the two layers of bread. Bake in a 400 degree F oven until crisp.

8 ounces pitted Kalamata olives, rinsed in cool water

2 tablespoons slivered almonds

3 tablespoons coarsely chopped fresh basil leaves

1¹/₂ tablespoons fresh lemon juice

¹/₂ preserved lemon (see page 113)

2 tablespoons olive oil

Freshly ground black pepper to taste

Put all the ingredients in a food processor and blend until they form a smooth paste.

Marinated Fish with Fried Vermicelli
(Serves 4 to 6 as an appetizer)

¹/₂ pound fillet firm, mild-flavored fish such as tilapia or flounder

1 teaspoon Dijon mustard

¹/₂ cup fresh lemon juice

¹/₂ cup fresh orange juice

2 tablespoons olive oil

1 tablespoon balsamic vinegar

1¹/₂ teaspoons salt

Freshly ground black pepper to taste

Vegetable oil for frying

About 20 Chinese rice noodles
(use flat noodles the width of linguine)

Salt to taste

Lemon slices

2 tablespoons chopped cilantro

Remove any skin from the fish and cut fillet into thin slices. In a nonreactive bowl large enough to hold the fish, mix the mustard, lemon and orange juices, olive oil, vinegar, salt, and pepper. Place the fish into this marinade and toss gently. Cover and refrigerate for six hours.

Just before serving, heat 1 inch of vegetable oil in a large, deep frying pan until a piece of noodle dropped into the pan immediately puffs up. Add a handful of the noodles. When puffed, remove with a slotted spoon and drain on paper towels, salting

Marinated Fish with Fried Vermicelli

lightly. Repeat with all the noodles. Arrange the noodles on a platter and place the fish slices on top. Garnish with halved lemon slices and chopped cilantro. Serve with Eggplant Caviar.

Eggplant Caviar

(Makes 2 cups)

1 ½ pounds eggplant (about 2 medium eggplants)

3 garlic cloves

1 lemon

½ teaspoon ground cumin

1 teaspoon sweet paprika

¼ teaspoon salt

Freshly ground black pepper to taste

1 small bunch fresh mint

4 tablespoons olive oil

Preheat the oven to 400 degrees F. Cut the garlic into slices. Make slits in the eggplants and force the garlic slices into the slits. Bake the eggplants on a baking sheet for 30 to 40 minutes, until soft. While the eggplant cools, zest and juice the lemon, reserving both juice and 1 teaspoon of zest. Scoop out the eggplant flesh and garlic slices and discard the skin. In a food processor, puree the eggplant with the cumin, paprika, salt, pepper, lemon juice, lemon zest, and 10 to 12 mint leaves. Slowly pour in the olive oil while pureeing the mixture. Chop the remaining mint leaves.

Serve the dip at room temperature garnished with the chopped mint.

79

Milan Meets Morocco

RIAD 72

Giovanna Cinel came to Marrakech for a holiday three years ago and stayed much longer than she planned. She also bought a *riad,* an activity that did not appear on her original agenda. "I was really fascinated by Marrakech—its small streets, the chaos at every time of day," she remembers. "There is something mysterious about the city that reminds me of Venice, which I know very well." A designer and photographer, Giovanna lives in Milan half of the year and resides in Marrakech for the remaining months where she now manages her *riad*—Riad 72—as a guesthouse. ⌀⌀ When she acquired it, the early-twentieth-century courtyard dwelling was in a state of ruin. Giovanna, like all foreigners who purchase Moroccan homes, was faced with the challenge of how to interpret the building—whether to renovate it traditionally or update it. She also had to decide how to integrate her own personal design preferences and cultural identity with the Moroccan structure. Working with Moroccan architect Karim El Achat, she took her first cues from the building itself.

OPPOSITE: *Dark aubergine* tadlekt *creates a dramatic backdrop for modernist furnishings in Riad 72's dining room, including a high-gloss tangerine table designed by Jasper Morrison.*

81

"We tried as much as possible to keep the historic structure in place," she explains, "retaining the original woodwork, carved plaster, and tile." By painting the plaster walls white and the woodwork a starkly contrasting shade of nearly black aubergine, Giovanna transformed the traditional courtyard into something clean-edged and modern. In keeping with this modern mood, she designed a sleek rectangular pool with a monolithic fountain of gray *tadlekt* in the center of the court. Giovanna, who professes a preference for serene, empty spaces, says, "When you walk into Riad 72, I want you to feel like you are entering a paradise of peace."

Giovanna also wanted to find a way to integrate a contemporary Italian design aesthetic with elements of Moroccan style. To achieve this, she imported several pieces of Italian furniture for a strikingly modern multi-use salon on the first floor. On one end of the room, contemporary wooden chairs with simple lines designed by Piero Lissoni surround a sharp-edged geometric table with a brilliant orange finish. Black consoles and a heavy black-framed mirror from Laboratorio Avallone Milano provide equally strong statements of unadorned geometry.

Giovanna echoes the color, symmetry, and simplicity of these furnishings in the surrounding space. *Tadlekt* in purplish-black and tangerine covers the lower portions of the walls and floor, creating a dramatic architectural setting. A bright red Berber rug provides more color, and light filters through pierced-metal Moroccan lamps. To complement the Italian furnishings, Giovanna designed a large cedar banquette that fills one wall of the large room in the Moroccan tradition. "All the things I've designed for the house are modern in line, but incorporate traditional Moroccan material: cedar, *tadlekt,* and local textiles."

Despite the high-contrast color scheme, this room maintains a serene tone, thanks to the purity of form and elegant symmetry of the decorations. A similar approach permeates the guest rooms as well. In one bedroom, a length of bright tie-dyed fabric hangs from the doorway and a funky lamp with a tall red shade recalls the mod mood of Morocco in the 1970s, when hippies from Europe and America discovered the country's charms. But a gray-and-white tile floor and a simple banquette of wood with plain canvas cushions tone down these wild-child details.

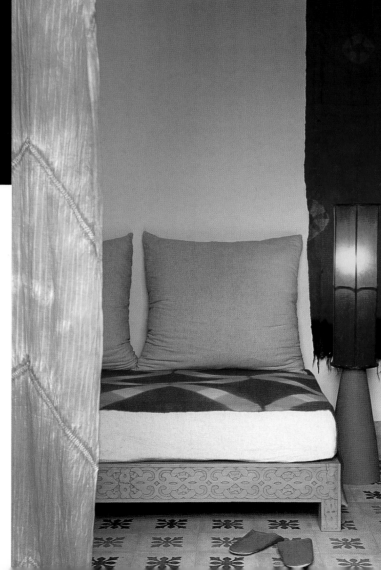

LEFT: *Integrated into the very contemporary salon, typical Moroccan elements including nubby Berber carpets and pierced metal lamps look as fresh and chic as the Italian furnishings they accompany.*

RIGHT: *The tie-dyed hangings of this bedroom suite, decorated in hippie-chic style, pay homage to the days when Jimi Hendrix and other psychedelic rockers hung out in Morocco.*

84

Another bedroom has much more of a typical Moroccan appearance, with its niches of hand-shaped plaster, *tagguebbast* details, and arched windows. And yet the severe simplicity of the furnishings—tall espresso-colored dressers flanking a low bed draped with a dramatic throw of tangerine velvet—transform the space into a peacefully modern retreat. "I prefer things to have simple shapes," says Giovanna. Her favorite place in the *riad* is actually the roof terrace, which is reached by climbing two flights of twisting, irregular stairs that wind through the dark, enclosed corners of the *riad*. One then finds the rooftop with a canopy of white fabric and low divans upholstered in heavy white canvas. From this vantage point, Giovanna enjoys studying the variety of *riads* that surround her own. "You can see a decadent, falling-down *riad* next to one that has been perfectly restored," she says. "And you appreciate the contrast between the anonymous exteriors of these buildings and their very individual interiors."

Giovanna declares, "It is important to do something that will remain in the future, to leave something new to the people who come." At Riad 72, she has left the distinctive mark of the new generation of Marrakechi–European and American expatriates who graft their own contemporary styles and cultural references on the already diverse foundation of Moroccan style.

ABOVE: *Banana trees and climbing vines create a cool sanctuary in the courtyard, where water quietly spills across the gray* tadlekt *surface of a minimalist fountain.*

Gogo Maroc

A MOROCCAN FEAST ON MARTHA'S VINEYARD

"If I'm going to throw a party, I'm really going to throw a party," exclaims Gogo Ferguson, jewelry designer, importer of Moroccan decorative objects, and hostess extraordinaire. Recently Gogo and her husband, David Sayre, created a new island retreat in Martha's Vineyard, where they live and entertain their friends during the summer months. "It looks like a typical New England cottage on the outside, with gray shingles and white mullioned windows," says Gogo, "but when you go inside, you feel like you're in Morocco." ᴄ—ꞷ Dave and Gogo got the idea of bringing Moroccan style back to the Vineyard five years ago after they visited North Africa on a belated honeymoon. "We were absolutely captivated by the colors, the crafts, and people's ability to transform anything, whether the carving around the door or a window grate, into marvelous designs," Gogo recalls. "We brought home carvings, wrought iron, and doors and came up with ways to incorporate them into our house." ᴄ—ꞷ Although Dave, a master carpenter, compares the original appearance of the modest 1950s house to a double-wide trailer,

OPPOSITE: *A dazzling table laden with Moroccan-inspired food and colorful late summer flowers create an enchanted atmosphere for a fusion party on Martha's Vineyard.*

the end result of this intensive renovation project bears no resemblance to a mobile home. Rustic beams now support a soaring ceiling in the living room. Massive carvings from a Moroccan doorway combine with a salvaged mantel to create a monumental fireplace. Casement windows from demolished Martha's Vineyard structures replace the house's original crank-out windows. The interior walls, once clad in cheap wood paneling, have been stripped and resurfaced with sunflower-yellow *tadlekt*.

It wasn't only the architecture and design of Morocco that made a strong impression on Gogo and Dave. Gogo also remembers in vivid detail the first Moroccan party she attended. "I couldn't open my eyes any wider. Every single one of my senses was dazzled by the food, the flowers, the sound of drumming in the background." The couple decided to host a Moroccan feast on the Vineyard when they got back from a recent trip to Marrakech during which they stocked up on Moroccan decorative objects to sell in their two boutiques: Gogo Maroc in Vineyard Haven and Gogo in Sea Island, Georgia.

Since Gogo and Dave have ready access to Moroccan decorative objects ranging from delicately tinted tea glasses to black-and-white Berber tents, it wasn't hard to create an authentic setting for the late-summer feast. While Dave hoisted the tents (a large one over the buffet table and a whimsical conical one for the bar), Gogo threw brightly colored cloths and Moroccan shawls over tables scattered about the yard. She decorated these with silver chargers and tea glasses, arranging centerpieces of the Vineyard's plentiful sunflowers in Moroccan serving dishes glazed deep shades of lapis lazuli, gold, and rust.

Throughout the house and yard, Gogo fused seasonal, regional elements with exotic Moroccan details. Locally grown beets, peppers, and gourds bought

LEFT: *Yellow sunflowers inspired the color of* tadlekt *that transforms the interior of this Martha's Vineyard house into a Moroccan-style retreat.*

OPPOSITE: *Moroccan wrought iron ornaments the balcony overlooking the living room; carved wooden door panels and* mousharabiya *add Moorish touches to the fireplace.*

BELOW: *Two Moroccan
tents decorated with the
black and white patterns
typical of nomadic Berber
tents create fanciful
shelters for the bar and
buffet.*

OPPOSITE: *Pillows uphol-
stered in fragments of
kilim and Berber rugs
transform the Martha's
Vineyard patio into a
colorful, sensual refuge.*

ABOVE: *A stream at the
back of the property gets
a Moroccan makeover
with a cascade of rose
petals and a flotilla of
lotus-bud-shaped candles.*

that morning at the farmers' market formed a centerpiece on the buffet table. The house's very Vineyard back porch, with its gray-and-white palette of shingles and slate, assumed the appearance of a Marrakech terrace once it was scattered with rugs and kilim-covered pillows, low brass tables, and glittering glasses and lamps. Even the stream at the back of the property received a Moroccan makeover when Gogo and friends set adrift candles shaped like lotus buds and scattered it with rose petals gathered from a garden once tended by Lillian Hellman.

For the feast, caterer Annie Foley also mixed and matched traditional Moroccan ingredients such as *harissa* and couscous with the fruits of the Vineyard's waters and fields: plump scallops and mussels, ripe tomatoes, and freshly picked corn. The result was a fusion feast that dazzled the senses: polenta stars drizzled with tomato chutney, mussels spiked with *harissa* sauce, succulent brochettes of halibut and lamb, steaming mounds of couscous studded with caramelized figs and nuts, and mountains of multicolored olives.

Cocktails of vodka, lemon juice, and soda spiked with mint from a neighbor's garden started off the evening. As the sun set, drummers beat their instruments beneath the trees and dancers emerged like flames from the shadows. Flaming torches and candles made the yard glow like the courtyard of a *kasbah*. The brightest spot, the colorfully laden buffet table, drew a steady stream of visitors until the last plates of cinnamon-dusted orange slices were emptied and the guests began to turn toward home.

OPPOSITE: *In a mood of Orientalist opulence, Gogo prepared a buffet table overflowing with food and flowers that combine the colors and flavors of Morocco and the Vineyard.*

Menu for a Moroccan Feast

Spicy Harissa Mussels in the Shell

Mock Polenta Stars with Moroccan Tomato Chutney, Chevre, and Mint

Scallop Brochettes with Charmoula Sauce

Halibut Brochettes with Mint Sauce*

Lamb, Tomato, and Red Onion Brochettes with Yogurt-Cumin Sauce*

Saffron-Scented Tagine of Potato, Okra, Green Beans, and Sweet Corn

Couscous with Caramelized Figs, Crushed Nuts, and Mint*

(Recipes begin on page 94)

*recipes not included

Spicy Harissa Mussels in the Shell

Heat the oil in an 8-quart pot over medium-high heat. Add the onions and sauté until golden. Add the garlic, ginger, and anchovy paste and cook for 2 minutes. Add the tomatoes, cream, *harissa* paste, and smoked paprika, and simmer for 5 minutes. Set aside to cool; then puree. (This sauce can be prepared up to a day ahead of time and refrigerated until ready to use.)

Reheat the sauce in the same pot and add the mussels to the heated mixture. Cover with a lid and cook for 8 to 10 minutes or until the mussels open. Stir once. Remove the mussels from the pan and take off the top shells, discarding any mussels that did not open. Arrange the mussels on a serving plate, drizzle with the sauce, and garnish with the parsley.

Spicy Harissa Mussels in the Shell
(Serves 10 as an appetizer or 4 as an entrée)

$^1/_2$ cup vegetable oil

1 medium onion, finely chopped

2 garlic cloves, minced

1 tablespoon grated peeled fresh ginger

1 teaspoon anchovy paste

2 tomatoes, finely chopped

$^1/_4$ cup heavy cream

$^1/_4$ cup *harissa* paste

2 teaspoons smoked paprika

4 dozen mussels, scrubbed and debearded

Chopped parsley for garnish

Mock Polenta Stars with Moroccan Tomato Chutney, Chevre, and Mint
(Makes about 50 stars)

2 cups uncooked quick grits

2 cups Moroccan Tomato Chutney (recipe follows)

2 logs (8 ounces each) mild goat cheese, at room temperature

Fresh mint leaves, chopped, for garnish

Preheat the oven to 350 degrees F.

Prepare the grits according to the package directions. While grits are cooking, grease 2 baking sheets with raised edges. Spread the cooked grits in a quarter-inch layer on the greased baking sheets and cool. When the grits are cool, cut out stars using a star-shaped cookie cutter. (The stars can be baked at once or kept layered between sheets of waxed paper in an airtight container in the refrigerator until ready to brown in the oven.)

Place the stars on greased baking sheets. Placing 1 baking sheet into the oven at a time, cook the stars for 5 minutes or until slightly golden and crisp on top.

Arrange the crisped stars on a platter and drizzle each star with a heaping teaspoon of warm Moroccan Tomato Chutney. Add a small dollop of goat cheese to each star and garnish with chopped mint.

Moroccan Tomato Chutney
(Makes about 2 cups)

8 ounces sliced, peeled ginger

1 cup cider vinegar

2 quarts cherry tomatoes, halved

2 cups (loosely packed) dark brown sugar

2 cups granulated sugar

2 lemons, sliced and seeded

1 tablespoon ground cinnamon

1 tablespoon ground cumin

1 teaspoon ground cloves

¼ teaspoon cayenne pepper (or to taste)

1 teaspoon salt

1 teaspoon freshly ground black pepper

1 cup water

In a large, heavy pan, combine the ginger, vinegar, tomatoes, sugars, lemons, and spices with the water. Bring to a boil. Reduce heat to medium-low and cook, stirring occasionally, for 2 hours until the sauce reduces and thickens to a chutney consistency. Remove the lemon and ginger and keep sauce warm until ready to serve. This sauce can be made ahead and refrigerated for several days in a nonreactive storage container.

Mock Polenta Stars

Scallop Brochettes with Charmoula Sauce
(Makes 10 brochettes)

2¹/₂ pounds large sea scallops (about 50 scallops)

¹/₂ cup olive oil

¹/₄ cup fresh lemon juice

Salt and freshly ground black pepper to taste

1 cup Charmoula Sauce (recipe follows)

Prepare the grill or preheat the broiler. In a large non-reactive bowl, toss the scallops with the oil, lemon juice, and salt and pepper. Arrange the scallops on skewers (about 5 scallops per skewer) and grill, turning once, for a total of 5 minutes or until they are lightly browned on both sides. Serve hot, drizzled with Charmoula Sauce, with additional sauce on the side.

Charmoula Sauce
(Makes about 1 cup)

4 garlic cloves

¹/₂ medium onion

2 teaspoons ground cumin

1¹/₂ teaspoons sweet paprika

³/₄ teaspoon ground turmeric

¹/₄ teaspoon salt

¹/₂ cup fresh cilantro, coarse stems removed

¹/₃ cup flat-leaf parsley, coarse stems removed

7 tablespoons extra-virgin olive oil

7 tablespoons lemon juice

Freshly ground black pepper to taste

Place the garlic and onion in a food processor and pulse until coarsely chopped. Add the spices, salt, cilantro, parsley, oil, and lemon juice and process until the ingredients achieve the texture of a thin pesto. Adjust salt and add pepper to taste.

Saffron-Scented Tagine of Potato, Okra, Green Beans, and Sweet Corn
(Serves 10)

2 tablespoons olive oil

2 medium onions, thinly sliced

1 pound fresh tomatoes, chopped
(or 1 16-ounce can whole tomatoes)

30 sprigs fresh flat-leaf parsley, tied with cotton string

15 sprigs fresh cilantro, tied with cotton string

2 cups water

10 threads Spanish saffron, toasted and crushed

1 teaspoon ground turmeric

2 teaspoons ground ginger

¹/₂ teaspoon salt

²/₃ pound small red-skinned potatoes, peeled and halved
(about 6 potatoes)

²/₃ pound okra, tough stems removed

²/₃ pound baby green beans

3 ears of sweet corn, sliced through the cob
to make $^1/_2$-inch-thick circles

Freshly ground black pepper to taste

Chopped fresh parsley for garnish

Chopped fresh cilantro for garnish

Heat the oil in a large pot over medium-high heat and sauté the onions for 5 minutes or until tender but not browned. Add the tomatoes, parsley, cilantro, and water, and bring to a boil. Cover and cook over medium-high heat for 10 minutes. Remove the parsley and cilantro bundles. Reduce the heat to medium. Add the saffron threads, turmeric, ginger, salt, potatoes, and okra. Cook, covered, for 30 minutes or until the potatoes and okra are tender. Add the green beans and corn and cook, covered, for 5 minutes or until the green beans and corn are tender. If sauce is too thin, remove the vegetables and boil the sauce until it is reduced and thickened. Adjust seasoning for salt and pepper, return vegetables to the sauce, and serve hot. Garnish with chopped parsley and cilantro.

Fresh hydrangea blooms are scattered across tables draped with Moroccan silk shawls and set with silver chargers and tea glasses from Morocco.

minimalism

TAKEN AS A WHOLE, THE LANGUAGE OF MOROCCAN STYLE

can seem overwhelming, yet when allowed to stand alone the individual elements of the country's architecture, design, and cuisine reveal an elegant, pure, elemental quality. Crisply geometric patterns of blue-and-white *zellij*, sun-bleached panels of carved cedar, rhythmic arcades of white plaster, sinuous lines of wrought-iron balconies: each reveals the hand of a master craftsperson and the beauty of refined materials. Dazzling feasts can also be broken down into simply perfect single dishes: carrots tossed with fresh herbs and spices, fish coated with spices and quickly seared, orange sections garnished with slivered dates and almonds.

While Moroccan style means "more is better" to many, there is a new generation of designers, architects, chefs, hoteliers, and homeowners who recognize that less can definitely be more. Some of these minimalists look to the countryside for inspiration, rediscovering the robust, earthy materials from which Moroccans have built structures for more than two thousand years: the pounded red earth *pisé* of *kasbahs* and *ksour*; handmade bricks; stone and mortar; rustic wooden beams. Others reinterpret the more urban Andalusian style by simplifying its polychromatic palette and busy patterns. Still others turn to nature for inspiration, celebrating the elemental colors and textures of earth, sky, and water, of metal, wood, and undyed cloth.

These newcomers are redefining Moroccan style, bringing a contemporary aesthetic to bear on age-old materials and techniques. While some say that they are tapping into the most authentic expression of ancient Moroccan style, others claim to be staking out new territory, adding yet another layer of expression to an already highly stratified style. By drawing undivided attention to the clear beauty of the building blocks of Moroccan architecture and cuisine, these minimalists demonstrate the timeless appeal and ultimate versatility of Moroccan style.

Meditation in Gray and White

DAR KAWA

The path to Dar Kawa, a seventeenth-century *riad* in the heart of the Marrakech medina, zigzags through narrow streets that are saturated with color: red *pisé* walls punctuated with bright green, blue, and yellow doors; *souks* where the brilliant wares of artisans are displayed; and open-air shops piled high with mounds of bright fruit and plastic-wrapped candies. In stark contrast to this visual cacophony, a mood of order prevails behind the walls of Dar Kawa, where the only tones are gray and white and the architecture and furnishings express a serene geometry. ⁓ By minimizing color and surface decoration, Belgian architect Quentin Wilbaux emphasizes the essential elegance of Dar Kawa's architecture. The courtyard, paved entirely in gray tile, becomes a mesmerizing meditation on the beauty of shape and line. Square and rectangular tiles arranged in alternating bands of monochromatic pattern spread out across the floor. The archetypal Islamic garden form—four trees surrounding a central fountain—becomes abstract when translated into four small sunken beds surrounding a low bowl of marble filled with burbling water.

OPPOSITE: *The gray and white palette allows the architectural details of the seventeenth-century* riad, *including arches with a range of complex silhouettes, to reveal their intricacies.*

OPPOSITE: *Rough-hewn wooden stools, typical of nomadic furniture, share a corner with a contemporary steel chair designed by former sculptor Frederic Butz.*

Instead of the open colonnades that typically surround *riad* courtyards, solid walls of whitewashed plaster enclose Dar Kawa's central court. But these are rendered transparent by large openings that celebrate the infinite variety of the arch. Two giant arches square off across the courtyard, towering the full height of the two-story structure. These arches frame the walls behind them, which are also pierced with apertures including an intricately cusped arch shaped like the jagged entrance to a cave.

With its monochromatic simplicity, the architecture of the building invites undistracted contemplation of texture and material: gray-washed wooden doors and beams; sand-colored carved plaster; glossy glazed tile on the courtyard floor; and the warm, matte glow of unglazed earthenware tile on the roof above. Within this setting, the senses become highly attuned to detail. Canvas-clad butterfly chairs and Moroccan carved octagonal wooden tables—familiar furniture classics that might disappear in a busier environment—assume new dignity.

Valérie Barkowski, an entrepreneur who operates the Marrakech Medina network of guesthouses, also fills the rooms and terraces with contemporary designs. While restoring Dar Kawa as a guesthouse, she commissioned several of the hottest young designers working in Marrakech to create unique furniture, linens, and ceramics to complement the *riad*'s minimalist aesthetic. Frederic Butz, a French artist turned furniture designer, made the stainless steel chairs, beds, and bathroom fixtures that lend an air of industrial chic to the rooms. While the material is distinctly non-Moroccan, the shapes of the furniture—sweeping arcs, flat planes pierced with round openings, and towel racks in an updated interpretation of the ancient Fatima's hand—make both subtle and overt references to Moroccan design.

Barkowski herself designed the crisply modern bed linens that play with Moroccan references; their miniature tassels recall the ornamentation of traditional Moroccan robes called *djellebahs*. Some beds are dressed entirely in white, while others incorporate touches of blue and red as accents to the white surroundings. An occasional Moroccan lamp with colored glass panes, a woven rug with subtle earth-red patterning, and sepia-toned photographs provide just enough

ABOVE: *Tiles in a variety of shapes and shades of gray create an elegantly monochromatic surface.*

RIGHT: *The sweeping arc of a steel bed frame designed by Butz echoes arches framing the courtyard outside the bedroom door.*

OPPOSITE: *Tagine-shaped serving dishes, designed by Charlotte Barkowski, complement Dar Kawa's minimalist elegance.*

relief from the prevailing palette to prevent it from crossing the line into austerity.

When a welcoming cup of mint tea is served, guests realize that their hostess has focused her finely tuned minimalist aesthetic on even the smallest detail. The white glazed tea set designed by Barkowski's stepdaughter, Charlotte Barkowski, with its playful sense of scale—tall teapot, tiny sugar bowl—has the timeless elegance of Cycladic figurines. Even in the kitchen, the same rigorous aesthetic is at work. White *tagines* designed to match the *riad*'s dinner service are stacked in floor-to-ceiling shelves. Gray glazed tiles cover the floor, their soft sheen echoed by the stainless steel counter and backsplash that provides an attractive and utilitarian work surface.

Gray and white are the colors of shadow and light. For this reason, Barkowski's carefully selected furnishings take on an elemental quality when arranged on the open-air roof terrace. The white canvas slings of the butterfly chairs shimmer like wings in the afternoon sun. The glossy surface of a steel table gleams like the undisturbed surface of a pool of water. The din from the streets below, where donkey carts and mopeds vie for precious room along the crowded streets, disperses before it reaches the *riad*'s serene terrace. Here, the focus is on the color of the sky, the flight of birds, and the distant cry of the muezzin who reminds the faithful to lift their thoughts beyond this world to the realm of pure spirit. Although a visit to Dar Kawa cannot promise access to that other realm, it does invite meditation and inspire appreciation for the simple beauties of this one.

OPPOSITE: *The delicate lines of wrought-iron window screens stand out in sharp contrast to the spare white surroundings.*

BELOW: *Bed linens ornamented with tiny tassels and pompoms inject a subtle note of whimsy into the sophisticated bedrooms.*

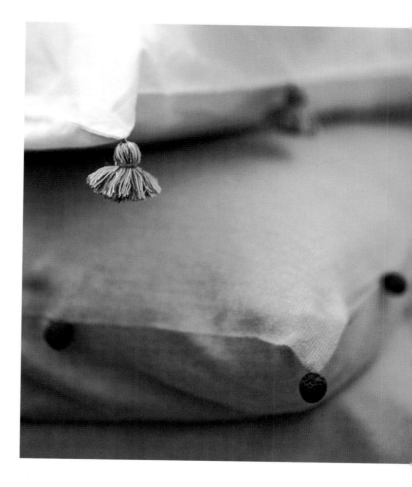

A Celebration of the Senses

AMANJENA

The goal of minimalist architecture, design, and cuisine is not to minimize sensation but rather to concentrate the senses by diminishing distraction. Color is unified. Pattern is simplified. Texture is toned down. Flavor is purified. Suddenly, an architectural element that has been seen many times before in a crowded environment assumes new elegance and grandeur. Or a spice mixture that has been tasted again and again, surprises and delights the palate when allowed to shine in an uncomplicated preparation. Interpreted in this spirit, minimalism becomes a celebration of the elements and the senses with which we experience them. This is the kind of minimalism that Amanresorts founder Adrian Zecha and American architect Ed Tuttle had in mind when they created Amanjena. The architect drew inspiration from Morocco's rich building tradition, specifically the colonnaded courtyards of *riads* and palaces, the earthy walls of desert *kasbahs,* and the vaulted prayer halls of mosques. At Amanjena, aspects from these traditions have been magnified, intensified, and married to the essential elements of the Moroccan landscape: red earth, cool water, clear light, and desert wind.

OPPOSITE: *The entrance hall at Amanjena is a cavernous arcade of sun-paled red horseshoe arches that frame views of the resort's lush courtyards.*

OVERLEAF: *Rose-colored pavilions encircle a large* bassin, *one of many water elements that cool the air and soothe the ears and eyes of the palatial resort's guests.*

108

ABOVE: *Ed Tuttle, the resort's architect, designed tableware that reflects his minimalist approach to shape, color, and line.*

Earth and straw are blended to make the *pisé* walls that encircle the resort located in a date palm grove at the base of the Atlas Mountains. Water from the melted snow of the mountains reflects the sky in a giant *bassin*. Light plays in the entrance hall, accentuating the arabesque silhouettes of a vast arcade of horseshoe arches. Fires blaze at night in massive fireplaces and candles twinkle in myriad lanterns that are placed at twilight throughout the grounds.

The setting awakens each of the five senses. The fragrance of roses fills the air, exuding from giant bouquets and the scattered petals that float in fountains. A subtle color scheme dominated by sun-paled red—a hue inspired by nearby Marrakech, which is called "the red city"—delights the eyes. Rooftops of glazed green tile and canals lined with turquoise *zellij* provide cool contrast.

Glossy columns of marble and onyx, soft suede upholstery, and ceramic tiles that absorb the sun's warmth delight the sense of touch. The burbling of fountains, the whisper of wind blowing against curtains, and the haunting cries of doves create a soothing background of ambient sound.

Taste buds are thrilled by the creations of executive chef Barnaby Jones, a versatile master of cuisine who has studied and worked in England, France, the Caribbean, and the Far East. Despite this eclectic background, Jones claims not to be a great lover of fusion cuisine, which he believes results all too often in overly seasoned, confusing concoctions. Yet Jones's menus reveal a distinct penchant for combining ingredients and ideas from varied culinary traditions. What separates this approach from what has become popularly known as fusion cuisine is Jones's subtlety and restraint.

Asked to create a romantic dinner for two that expresses Amanjena's Moroccan minimalist aesthetic, Jones's talents sparkle. The menu begins with a classic French terrine of foie gras that reveals Jones's understanding of flavor and his expertise with an international array of ingredients. "Foie gras is very rich and requires something acidic to balance it," he explains. "In this case, I use Moroccan preserved lemons mixed with almond paste."

This appetizer is followed by Jones's reinterpretation of Morocco's ubiquitous cooked vegetable salads. By minimizing the spices, he focuses attention upon the natural flavor, color, and texture of pale green artichoke hearts, fresh fava beans, and lightly poached carrots.

For the main course, seared red mullet rubbed with *charmoula* paste, Jones again combines ingredients and preparations from France and Morocco. While the traditional Moroccan preparation of fish in *charmoula* calls for lengthy cooking until the fish is flaky and tender, Jones prefers the crisp skin and firm flesh of fish that has been quickly seared. He arranges the crisp fillets on a golden ragout of new potatoes and olives that have been slow-cooked in a turmeric-laced sauce.

For dessert, Jones steers clear of gustatory pyrotechnics in favor of simple, flavorful ingredients, preparing a salad of sliced oranges, toasted almonds, and slivered dates. Served with refreshing Moroccan mint tea under the pale light of the rising moon, this final course leaves the palate singing and the diners sated, wishing that their days in paradise might never end.

Preserved Lemons
(Makes 8)

Preserved lemons require a minimum of 3 weeks to cure, but they will keep, refrigerated, for up to 6 months.

8 firm, thin-skinned organic lemons, scrubbed

10 tablespoons sea salt or kosher salt

4 cups water

Cut a small circle of skin off the top and bottom of each lemon. Turn each lemon on its base and slice three-quarters of the way through it vertically. Turn the lemons over and make a second slice three-quarters of the way through at a 90-degree angle to the first slice. Pack each cut with salt, reserving 2 tablespoons of salt. Push the salted lemons into one or more sterilized jars. Bring the water to a boil and add the 2 remaining tablespoons of salt. Pour this brine into the jars to cover the lemons. Put a double layer of plastic wrap over the top of each jar and seal with a lid. Cure at room temperature for 2 to 3 weeks, until the peels are soft and the pulp is gooey.

Seared Red Mullet
with Charmoula Paste
(Serves 4)

3 tablespoons olive oil

2 tablespoons fresh lemon juice

1 tablespoon chopped fresh parsley

2 garlic cloves, minced

1 teaspoon ground cumin

1/2 teaspoon paprika

1/2 tablespoon ground coriander seed

1 teaspoon tomato paste

1/2 teaspoon salt

Freshly ground black pepper to taste

1 pound red mullet fillets (8 small fillets), skin on

Place the oil, lemon juice, parsley, garlic, cumin, paprika, coriander, tomato paste, salt, and pepper into a blender and puree into a smooth paste. Adjust for salt and pepper.

Place the fish fillets in a medium, flat non-reactive dish and spread with the marinade. If necessary, add 1 to 2 tablespoons of water in order to thin the marinade to the consistency of a thick sauce that clings to the fillets. Cover with plastic wrap and refrigerate for 2 hours.

Just before serving, heat a large nonstick sauté pan over medium-high heat. Place the marinated fillets skin side down in the hot pan (do not remove any *charmoula* paste that clings to the fish). When the skin is crisp, turn the fillet and cook for a minute longer.

Stack two fillets in the center of each plate and surround with New Potato Ragout with Olives (recipe follows).

Seared Red Mullet with Charmoula Paste on
New Potato Ragout with Olives

New Potato Ragout with Olives
(Serves 4)

3 tablespoons olive oil

1 medium onion, chopped

3 garlic cloves, minced

1 pound ripe tomatoes, peeled, seeded, and diced

1 teaspoon tomato paste

2 teaspoons ground cumin

$^1/_2$ teaspoon paprika

$^1/_2$ teaspoon ground turmeric

$^1/_2$ teaspoon salt

Freshly ground black pepper to taste

$^1/_4$ cup water

1 pound small red-skinned potatoes, peeled and halved
(about 8 potatoes)

2 tablespoons chopped fresh parsley

1 tablespoon chopped fresh cilantro

3 ounces pitted Kalamata
or other black olives, rinsed with cool water

$^1/_2$ preserved lemon, pulp reserved and zest julienned

In a large sauté pan, heat the oil over medium heat until shimmering. Add the onion and garlic and cover, cooking gently for 5 minutes, stirring occasionally until translucent. Add the tomatoes, tomato paste, cumin, paprika, turmeric, salt, pepper, and water. Cook over medium heat for 20 minutes until the sauce has reduced and thickened. Add the potatoes and additional water as needed to just cover the potatoes. Cover tightly and simmer slowly over medium-low heat for 30 minutes or until the potatoes are tender. Five minutes before the end of the cooking time, stir in the parsley, cilantro, olives, and preserved lemon pulp and zest and simmer uncovered until the pan juices thicken.

Orange and Date Salad
(Serves 4)

Juice of 1 orange

1 teaspoon orange flower water

$1^1/_2$ tablespoons confectioners' sugar

4 oranges, divided into segments

6 large dates, pitted and cut into slivers

$^3/_4$ teaspoon cinnamon

2 teaspoons almonds, toasted and crushed

In a medium nonreactive bowl, create a marinade by whisking together the orange juice, orange flower water, and 1 tablespoon of the confectioners' sugar. Add the orange segments and cover with plastic wrap. Refrigerate overnight or for a minimum of 6 hours. When ready to serve, use a slotted spoon to lift the orange segments out of the juices and arrange the orange segments with date slivers on each plate. Mix the toasted almonds with the cinnamon and remaining sugar. Scatter over the top of the fruit.

Moorish Hacienda

JNANE TAMSNA

"What I had in mind when I designed Jnane Tamnsa was to create a Moorish style hacienda," explains the resort villa's architect, interior designer, and proprietor, Meryanne Loum-Martin. While this fusion of Mexican and Moroccan style might at first sound a bit unexpected, it quickly makes sense as you stroll through the villa's stucco arcades, shady patios, and surrounding garden filled with flowering trees and palms. "Coming to Jnane Tamsna is like visiting a big country house surrounded by a farm," Meryanne elaborates, referring to her husband Gary Martin's organic garden and the natural *palmeraie* landscape that surrounds her newest resort outside of Marrakech. ⌒⌣ All the rooms frame views of the garden or the rural landscape of the walled enclave. At lunch and dinner, guests often eat herbs and vegetables from the garden while Gary dashes in with an update about a new plant he has successfully cultivated (an ethnobotanist, he is studying native plants and organic growing techniques). After meals, friends and

OPPOSITE: *In the living room at Jnane Tamsna, Meryanne Loum-Martin strikes the perfect balance between opulent surfaces and textures and a minimalist approach to color and shape.*

OPPOSITE: *The entrance invokes the serene simplicity of prayer hall architecture, where soaring horseshoe arches define a series of interconnected spaces.*

guests enjoy strolling through the grounds and learning about the age-old techniques of gardening Gary practices.

"At first I wondered, how do you feature an organic garden in a resort that is elegant and chic?" Gary muses. "We planted the garden before the house was built, and then we realized that it was absolutely beautiful!" In fact, Gary is so impressed with the appearance of the herbs and vegetables he has cultivated that many of them, including artichokes and bouquets of aromatic herbs, have found their way inside the villa's courtyard.

While the shape of the villa, with a pair of long wings enclosing a rectangular courtyard, is indeed reminiscent of hacienda architecture, the style of Jnane Tamsna is pure Loum-Martin chic. Meryanne designed boldly geometric furniture of cedar, bronze, and iron that incorporates her wide range of North African influences. But her sense of color has changed since she created Dar Tamsna, and a new minimalism has crept into her decors. "The new Moroccan style is about light colors and a more subtle, almost Zen-like approach to the fusion of African and Moroccan elements," she explains.

This new serene aesthetic is immediately evident at Jnane Tamsna. The entrance opens into a long arcade of horseshoe arches inspired by the architecture of Islamic prayer halls. The stucco is tinted in complementary tones of sun-paled gold and faded terra-cotta. Massive amphorae of varying shades of chalk and clay lean against the walls. Antique doors stripped of their polychrome paint open into spacious bedrooms painted a palette of light earth tones and herbal shades of lavender and sage. "Jnane Tamsna is located in a village called Douar Abiad, which means 'white village,'" Meryanne says, revealing the inspiration for the villa's pale palette. "The earth really is a lighter color here than elsewhere in the *palmeraie.*"

In one room, darkly burnished furniture with upholstery in shades of aubergine provides contrast against a backdrop of cream-on-cream plaster walls. In another, grayish-blue walls provide the perfect foil for colorful prints of African animals and a Moroccan rug with an earthy red background. Another guest room decorated almost entirely in a suede-inspired shade of beige relies not on color but on sculptural details for contrast. A gleaming *tadlekt* fireplace swells out from one

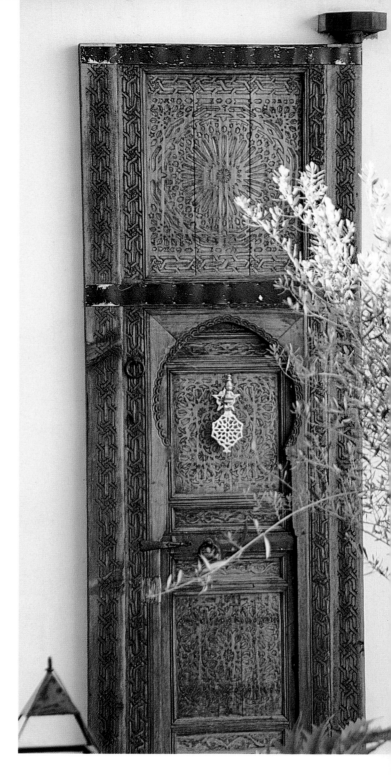

ABOVE: *A woven straw chair designed by Reda Bouamrani, a wooden chest, and darkly patinaed metal bring a spectrum of natural color into this courtyard corner.*

RIGHT: *Antique carved doors open off the central courtyard into spacious guest rooms.*

OPPOSITE: *Furniture designed by Meryanne reveals her bold approach to scale and love of burnished metal. A large drawing by Philippe Deltour reveals the ongoing romance between French artists and Moroccan subject matter.*

wall and a simplified interpretation of the Islamic eight-point-star motif is carved into the plaster cornice molding.

In the grand salon, Meryanne employs a warmer color scheme with muted terra-cotta *tadlekt* walls, fireplaces outlined with earth bricks, and kilims striped in vibrant red and orange shades. Even with the addition of Syrian chests with busy surfaces of mother-of-pearl inlay to Meryanne's sparer furniture designs, the room maintains a well-modulated mood, never crossing over into the heavy and overdecorated. Meryanne's unified approach to color contributes to the serenely dignified appearance of the room, but her bold attitude to scale is an even more important factor.

"Clutter is the enemy of balance," she opines. "When I design things, whether it is a chaise longue or a large bronze vessel, I like it to be large enough that it makes its own statement. It is better not to go halfway." This approach to design, which incorporates traditional Moroccan elements with more modern attitudes about scale, material, and decoration, helps to explain the enduring popularity of Meryanne's resorts with the international fashion set during the last fifteen years.

At Jnane Tamsna, Meryanne and Gary make every effort to share their vision with friends and clients and to encourage them to take home more than memories. While they stay, guests can absorb design and gardening lessons from their surroundings. When they depart, they can order furniture, accessories, and even the Dar Tamsna china pattern and a new line of linens that complement it. "At Jnane Tamsna, we mix traditional and unfamiliar elements to create a new kind of Moroccan fusion that reflects who we are and what we care about," Meryanne explains. "I want to encourage my guests to do the same when they return home."

OPPOSITE: *Meryanne's furnishings and textiles grace the bedrooms.*

ABOVE: *Antique prints of wildlife pay homage to Gary Martin's commitment to nurturing North Africa's natural resources.*

123

Stone Age Modern

EL CHERQUÏ

Nancy Bridger, a transplanted Californian who now lives atop an arid, rocky hill near Essaouira, loves to talk about her new neighbors. "Many of these families have only one camel and one donkey, so when they plow they harness them together to a wooden plow that hasn't changed much since the Stone Age," she relates. "One day I was driving into town and I saw an old man wearing a *djellebah* and a turban plowing a field with his donkey and camel. He looked like something out of ancient history, but when he reached the side of the road, I realized that he was talking away on his cell phone!" ∽ This blend of the ancient and the modern, the primitive and the civilized, is exactly what drew Nancy to Morocco and inspired her to create her Stone Age–modern retreat in a small farming village fifteen kilometers outside of Essaouira. "I love the colonial look, that overlay of some kind of Western society, whether English, or French, or Spanish, with a great undercurrent of something primitive and alien," she explains. "That hint of *eau de sauvage*."

OPPOSITE: *A cascade of red silk and a marble sculpture by American artist Stephen Angell add notes of refined elegance to the elemental atmosphere of Nancy Bridger's restored stone farmhouse.*

LEFT: *Inspired by the concept of constructing a domicile from the raw materials at hand, Bridger made a dining table out of rough planks and beams that served as scaffolding during restoration.*

BELOW: *El Cherquï, like most of the neighboring houses, is built from the stones and sandy soil of the land upon which it stands.*

Three years ago, Nancy sold her house in Malibu Lake, California, and put all her possessions in storage, setting out on a journey to an undetermined destination. "I wanted to change my whole life," she says. Her travels took her to Martinique, Paris, and the French countryside, where she nearly bought a house. Ultimately she arrived in Morocco. "I was staying with some friends who had just returned from Morocco," she recalls. "When I picked them up at the train station, sand was trickling out of their suitcases. I picked some of it up in my hands and said to myself, 'This is African sand. This is Moroccan sand.' And I followed that sand trail here."

Nancy first found herself in Ouarzazate, an ancient trading outpost on the boundary between the Atlas Mountains and the Sahara desert where warlords built *kasbahs*. When she toured other parts of the country, she discovered that the more-refined Andalusian architecture of the urban areas did not intrigue her. "It's so busy, so charged," she explains. When she decided to look at real estate in the area surrounding Essaouira, a small city on the Atlantic coast, she was captivated by the ruined shell of an old stone house that stood on top of a lonely hill.

It was the pure physical nature of the building that enthralled her. "Every stone in this house comes out of the ground it is built on," she exclaims. "The mortar is made from the sand of this hill mixed with water and a little bit of cement. To have a home built out of the very ground it stands on is practically a mystical experience."

By the time Nancy acquired the house, which she named El Cherquï in honor of the east wind that sweeps across the hill's summit, it was in a state of deterioration. The ceiling was gone and several of the interior walls were missing. But she could see where the original walls once stood and how tall the ceiling of the one-story structure had been. With the help of local workers, she began restoring the house and transforming it into a sensually rustic retreat.

Nancy maintained the original floor plan and used only traditional building materials for the main body of the house: stones from the property, sand, and cement. She added several modern details as well, including tall windows and a skylight to bring more sunlight into the house. She also added giant glass doors

protected by metal louvered shutters that lend a contemporary appearance to the facade and frame a view of the surrounding countryside.

When it came to decorating, Nancy decided to fashion furniture from building materials that had been used in the reconstruction of the house. She turned eucalyptus beams that had served as temporary supports for the ceiling into a four-poster bed and transformed raw planks used for scaffolding into banquettes and a table. Leather hassocks, chairs of wood and woven grass, and a collection of hand-thrown, hand-painted ceramics—all in tones of sand and earth—complement these designs.

Only a few elements of luxury offer contrast in color, texture, and mood. Gracefully contoured sculptures of satin-smooth marble created by Nancy's expatriate neighbor, American sculptor Stephen Angell, provide refined counterpoint to the craggy texture of the natural stone walls. A curtain of paprika-red silk cascades over the French doors opening into the house. "I was looking for something in saffron, but when I saw that color, I said, 'Yes! Yes!'" Nancy recalls. A duvet filled with feathers covers the wood bed and bright crimson mules decorated with more feathers lie where they have been tossed on the dressing room floor—remnants of Western extravagance in this ruggedly primitive retreat.

A set decorator who has worked on many Hollywood films and television movies and an interior designer with an international clientele, Nancy is adept at translating abstract visions into concrete, if often fleeting, reality. At El Cherquï, using little more than sticks and stones and her own fertile imagination, she has conjured from the dry earth her *eau de sauvage* dream. "As Americans, we tend to live in our fantasies," Nancy muses. "In Morocco, we are allowed to live in our greatest fantasy."

Maghreb Minimalism

RIAD MABROUKA

"The spirit of Africa flows in our veins," says Pierre-Jean Néri, who with his wife, Catherine, owns and operates Riad Mabrouka as a fashionable Marrakech guesthouse. While Pierre-Jean traces his African roots to Martinique, Catherine proudly claims a North African grandmother named Mabrouka who came from a Tuareg tribe in southern Algeria. Raised by a French doctor in a desert mission, this grandmother learned French language and manners at a young age and met and married a French officer in Fez during the early years of the protectorate. Although Pierre-Jean and Catherine lived for many years in France, they answered the call of their African roots two years ago, traveling through several North African cities until finally deciding to call Marrakech home. "Marrekech is the perfect combination of European cosmopolitanism and African exoticism," Catherine exclaims. The couple was also drawn to the city by the architecture of its *riads,* especially the intimately proportioned courtyard dwelling they chose as their home and guesthouse. "All the Oriental dreams can be found in this house," says Pierre, summing up his passion for the building's charms.

OPPOSITE: *A contemporary interpretation of* mousharabiya *designed by Catherine Néri incorporates an hourglass form common in Berber and Tuareg wooden implements. The screen provides a view into the entrance hall where photographs of Catherine's Tuareg grandmother, Mabrouka, hang upon the wall.*

133

The nineteenth-century *riad* is a classic expression of the Moroccan form. On two floors, long rooms surround a central courtyard where arches rise to form a white arcade. Two entertaining rooms—a dining room on the first floor and a living room on the second—still bear traces of the original polychrome plaster and wood. With the help of architect Christophe Siméon, the Néris designed new architectural details that betray a more modern approach to Moroccan style. They also decorated the rooms in a restrained, contemporary style using furnishings designed by Catherine, who translated a spectrum of North African influences ranging from the Tuareg to the French colonial into their minimalist essence.

An introduction to the couple's refined fusion style begins in the entrance hall—a small space enclosed by white plaster walls. Within one of these walls a narrow window opens onto a staircase. This window is decorated with a contemporary interpretation of *mousharabiya* in which the typically elaborate form of the carved wooden screen is purified into a simple geometric pattern. "This screen is inspired by the carvings on Berber and Tuareg wooden implements and furniture," Catherine explains, pointing to a collection of hand-carved tent pegs made by nomadic people that is displayed throughout the *riad*'s halls. A console table standing in the entrance hall beneath a selection of sepia-toned photographs of Mabrouka and her family incorporates the same geometric motif.

Wooden armchairs inscribed with cross-hatchings inspired by traditional Berber furniture from Meknès and the Middle Atlas are scattered among the rooms. Slender table lamps with parchment shades are similarly decorated, and a large floor lamp with an X-shaped base adopts the simplest of these geometric motifs as its overall form. These lamps share space in the second-floor salon with a cocktail table pierced with arabesque arches and deep-seated armchairs inspired by the furniture of the French Protectorate.

In this room, a carved plaster frieze and window niches glow in tones of malachite, lapis lazuli, and gold—remnants of the highly charged Andalusian style that once characterized the *riad*. A ceiling of age-darkened cedar offers another taste of the ornamental style favored by Thami El Glaoui, the early-twentieth-century pasha of Marrakech who reputedly owned this house. A simple fireplace

LEFT: *A diaphanous length of pale gray silk weighed at the corners with dark gray tassels forms a minimalist canopy in this bedroom decorated with furnishings designed by Catherine.*

of handmade brick and a palette of cream and white plaster offset these Moorish flourishes.

This balancing of overtly decorative North African details with spare furnishings and toned-down color permeates all the rooms at Riad Mabrouka. One suite is decorated entirely in shades of gray and white. While the room's windows and ceiling are fashioned from heavily carved cedar, the furnishings of iron are minimally embellished. The thinnest veil of gray silk hangs from the bed's iron canopy, weighted by four silk tassels. A wall of gray *tadlekt* in the bathroom beyond gleams like pewter. In another suite, stripes of ruby-red fabric sewn onto heavy canvas curtains and a diminutive slipper chair clad in red silk offer bright contrast to the neutral backdrop of ivory plaster.

Color takes center stage only on the rooftop terrace. Here, walls and a floor tinted deep ochre glow like sun-baked earth beneath the bright blue sky. The irregular roofline and surrounding walls creates a sculptural terrain of intersecting planes and shadows. The spirit of Mondrian and Le Corbusier seems to be hiding in the shadows of this unselfconsciously modern rooftop retreat, where the inherent minimalism of Moroccan architecture finds full expression. "I don't know if we are really modernists or if we are guided by our African blood," Catherine muses. "We just follow our instincts."

LEFT: *Original poly-chrome wood doors provide sumptuous counterpoint to the sophisticated minimalism.*

BELOW: *This raised bathtub has a wide edge that serves as a lavatory counter.*

delirium

"The . . . endless banquet at which course succeeded course—spiced chickens and pigeons, kous-kous, and whole roast sheep and kebab and almond pastries and sweet mint tea . . . lasted all through the night. Swaying lines of women danced to the music of their own wild chant; the traditional boy dancers, with painted faces and white robes drawn tight at the waist by gold-embroidered belts, danced to the tambourines and the clicking of the copper castanets on their fingers; in the courtyard a huge fire of juniper logs lit the battlements of the castle; outside the kasbah wall, . . . the night was loud with feasting."

GAVIN MAXWELL'S DESCRIPTION FROM LORDS OF THE ATLAS

of a feast lavished on the sultan of Morocco in 1893 by the politically ambitious Madani El Glaoui highlights the delirious extremes of hospitality for which Moroccans are famed. In his own palace in Fez, the early-twentieth-century sultan Moulay Abd El Aziz was reported by Maxwell to have "carved marble lions and living macaw parrots; jewels, real and false; steam-launches and fireworks; ladies' underclothing from Paris, and saddlery from Mexico; trees for gardens that were never planted, or, if planted, were never watered; printing-presses and fire balloons." ᴄᴧᴧᴡ Small wonder that artists and writers from the West sent home evocative images and accounts of the lavish and exotic scenes they encountered in Morocco's cities and remote mountain outposts. Today, Moroccan designers, homeowners, and hospitality entrepreneurs are equally inspired by the tradition of aesthetic and culinary excess, real and fantastic. Whether they live in an abandoned pasha's palace where echoes of past revelry fill empty courtyards; create new Orientalist resorts and restaurants where international clientele experience the sensual delights of Moroccan food, drink, and decor; or create private villas that explore the decorative trappings of the Moroccan dream, they are willing denizens of the delirious spell the country casts upon natives and foreigners alike.

House of Dreams

JAOUAD KADIRI'S PALMERAIE VILLA

In dreams, everything is simultaneously strange and familiar. We find ourselves easily navigating streets of cities we have never visited, encountering people we have known for years as well as strangers whom we recognize at once. Although some say we cannot dream in color, who hasn't awakened from a particularly vivid dream that was drenched in shades of Chinese red, cobalt blue, or sun-gold yellow? When architectural designer and nightclub owner Jaouad Kadiri collaborated with his friend and creative partner, expatriate American architect Stuart Church, the two succeeded in expressing the complex, kaleidoscopic nature of dreams in a luxurious villa on the outskirts of Marrakech. ᴔ To get to the villa, one must drive through the *palmeraie*—a large date palm grove where water lies waiting to be tapped beneath a rocky landscape. A route through this hard, red land leads to a wooden gate, beyond which spreads a garden filled with fountains, lotus-strewn pools, and flowery arcades. Visitors are greeted by a flock of tame geese who lead them to the front door with great politeness.

OPPOSITE: *The façade of Jaouad Kadiri's villa in the* palmeraie *outside Marrakech combines an Orientalist range of influences including Moroccan* kasbahs *and Indian palaces.*

140

LEFT: *This open-air living room is just one of many spaces that invite Jaouad and his guests to sit and savor the exotic beauty of the villa and its grounds. The furnishings, many of them designed by Jaouad and his friend, architect Stuart Church, combine Eastern influences with Victorian styles popular in the late nineteenth-century era of British colonialism.*

143

BELOW: *Ornamental details like this brass palmette tieback provide gleaming highlights in every room.*

OPPOSITE: *Twin hallways flank the soaring atrium.*

A mood of enchantment permeates the villa, cast by a combination of monumental scale (the ceiling of the living room is twenty meters high); archetypal shapes (stars, peacock tails, and palmetto fronds); intensely patterned fabrics; and overgrown vegetation cascading with pink, white, purple, and yellow blooms. Dream-friendly furniture is scattered throughout the U-shaped villa where divans command views of reflecting pools in open-air arcades, chaises longues invite the indolent visitor to recline, and a massive banquette has been known to accommodate twenty slumbering partyers after a particularly successful fete.

"This house is most magical at night," exclaims Jaouad, who loves to entertain. But one might easily argue for the beauty of daylight, when the sun swings around the pink stucco villa, filtering through *mousharabiya* screens and casting exotic shadows on the floors and walls as it passes through windows shaped like flowers, pointed arches, and even a perfume bottle.

"Every time you make an opening in a wall, you have a chance to shape it however you like," explains Stuart. "There is no reason to think that windows or doors have to be rectangular or square." The architect also demonstrates the infinite variety of the arch in Jaouad's house with tall Gothic arches, wide arches with hornlike cusps, and the scalloped arches that line a dramatic pair of halls. According to Stuart, long hallways can be boring, so he divided these up into rooms by using arches and hanging different lanterns in each space. The end result is reminiscent of the disorienting halls of Lewis Carroll's Wonderland, where young Alice wandered and wondered out loud, "Which way . . . which way?"

Throughout the villa, highly charged embellishments meet the eye—gleaming *tadlekt* walls in hot red, restful verdigris, and the soft color of sand. Painted doors and *mousharabiya* enliven entrances and windows. *Zellij* covers the floors and creeps up the walls and around the fireplaces. Boldly colored fabrics from India and Burma are randomly tossed over furniture and sewn into sumptuous covers for pillows and bolsters. Diaphanous canopies hang from the ceilings and raw silk curtains soften the walls. Richly patterned rugs cover the floors and silver, brass, and carved wooden and ceramic objects cluster on mantels and tabletops.

Jaouad and Stuart share a love of Oriental splendor and enjoy mixing the spoils of their travels and collecting sprees: brocades from the Gujarat region of India, puppets from Rajasthan, giant glass Christmas balls that reflect the influence of Byzantine and Venetian cultures, and ceramics with white-and-blue Persian designs. Other objects in the house are of their own invention. Tables and chairs designed by Jaouad and Stuart are inspired by Victorian furniture from England—a time when the English were incorporating exotic design lessons from their far-flung colonies.

"All the various Oriental influences are here," Stuart explains. "I don't think they can be divided and defined." As a rule, the architect avoids hard and fast definitions, preferring an ambiguous flow of ideas and of spaces. "I like the idea of transparency," he explains, "of being able to look through things." Jaouad's villa expresses this preference perfectly, with interior rooms opening onto arcades, which in turn frame views of the garden's long paths and shady grottos. Spiral staircases hidden in dark corners lead to a rooftop terrace where two giant rooms are housed in twin pavilions that frame views of the open sky. Elaborately decorated ceilings crown these rooms, competing with the star-strewn night sky in splendor.

Scattered with carpets, the floor of one of these suites is as fascinating as the faux-jewel-embellished ceiling above. "The colors are fantastic and the designs, so unpredictable," muses Jaouad as he admires an antique Berber rug. "The rug maker starts out at one point and ends up at another, as if he had forgotten where he had begun. There are all these strange things out of place—a camel here, a person there. It's impossible to make sense of it, which is what makes it so wonderful." This same capricious spirit fills the house, inviting Jaouad and his guests to lose their bearings and find themselves in an Orientalist dream.

OPPOSITE: *Yards upon yards of Indian and Burmese silk transform a four-poster bed into a sumptuous setting.*

ABOVE: *Transparency finds full expression in the lattice-lined loggias that face off across a water-garden.*

Moroccan Fantasy

RIAD ENIJA

The path to Riad Enija begins in the Place Jamaa El Fna, the bustling heart of Marrakech, where donkey carts, mopeds, motorcars, cyclists, and pedestrians hurl themselves in and around myriad shops, food stalls, and itinerant peddlers in a constant rush of coming and going. Congested streets lead away from this bustling plaza through the only slightly less hectic environs of a medina shopping area, terminating in a quiet residential street where children play and old men doze in the sun. A doorway opens at the end of this street, ushering guests into Riad Enija's exterior entrance hall—a narrow corridor enclosed by steep walls of thickly mortared bricks. The sounds of the city beyond are muffled within this transitional space. When the *riad*'s internal door opens, guests find themselves in a courtyard filled with towering tropical plants and spiny cactuses, the watery music of a fountain hidden amid the succulent growth, and a dizzying cacophony of birdsong. All the birds of Marrakech seem to have flocked to this lush oasis where they flit from branch to branch, uttering low cries and piercing shrieks.

OPPOSITE: *Bright pink, red, and orange satin upholstery create hot spots of color in the courtyard of Riad Enija, which is ornamented in the traditional Andalusian palette of blue and white.*

Turtles lumber silently along the paths of antique *zellij* in search of tender leaves, and chartreuse lizards blink slowly from their hideouts.

At Riad Enija, European hoteliers Ursula Haldimann and Björn Coerding have captured the pure fantasy of Marrakech and refracted it in a delirious kaleidescope of color, texture, and sound. A *caid*'s palace built nearly three hundred years ago and expertly remodeled in 1860 by a wealthy merchant from Fez, the *riad* is one of the more opulently detailed residences in Marrakech. Vast rooms decorated with multicolored mosaics, painted wood ceilings, and hand-carved plaster surround two courtyards. Deep verandas tucked behind columns offer shady vantage points from which to survey the beauty of the courtyards—the first, a plant-filled sanctuary for birds; the second, a serene paean to the elegance of Andalusian architecture.

Some find the visual richness of Andalusian design too overwhelming and try to tone it down by stripping away detail and subduing its polychrome palette. But Ursula found inspiration from the highly charged, exotic style of the *riad* she and her husband purchased and transformed into a guesthouse. Hot colors in a bouquet of tropical flower tones abound in the furnishings she selected for the verandas. Bright green and pink wicker chairs draped with scarves and pillows of magenta and rose cluster in corners around the garden courtyard. Elegant divans upholstered in red, hot pink, and bright orange satin perch among the blue-and-white *zellij* columns of the second courtyard.

"My style is very much my own," explains Ursula. "I try to match the strong colors where they fit, and I choose other colors in order to create the atmosphere that each room should have." With seven suites to decorate, she has succeeded in invoking the many moods of Moroccan fantasy, from fiery opulence fit for a pasha's party to dreamily serene escapes where windows frame blue fragments of sky and cloud.

Most rooms feature fanciful tasseled lanterns designed by Pier Lorenzo Salvoni from Carolyn Quartermaine silks. More silky fabrics drape the windows and cascade from the canopies that crown most of the beds. The furniture is a mix of traditional Moroccan pieces and contemporary European designs, including

OPPOSITE: *In this bedroom, shades of ivory and gold create an elegantly neutral backdrop for fanciful contemporary furniture.*

BELOW: *Rose petals in the courtyard fountain echo the flower tones of the sofas and chairs.*

minimalist divans, whimsical iron tables and chairs from Archangel (an English design firm), and an eccentrically embellished four-poster bed from French designer Chantal Saccomanno.

There is a timelessly surreal quality to these rooms—one decorated in cool tones of violet, another in softly gleaming shades of ivory, silver, and gold. Unexpected details, such as a sculpture of a brooding angel or a lightbulb surrounded by gauzy wings, tease the imagination. The rooms at Riad Enija are as much dreamscapes as they are retreats for rest and relaxation inviting those who visit them to write their own fanciful tales of *A Thousand and One Nights.*

LEFT: *Contrasts in colors and textures, and frequent interjections of the unexpected, create an atmosphere of surprise and delight at Riad Enija.*

OPPOSITE: *Ursula combines textiles from Carolyn Quartermaine (used in a pendant lamp designed by Pier Lorenzo Salvoni) and Brigitte Perkins to transform this small room into a dreamy hideaway.*

Sleeping Beauty

TEA IN THE GLAOUI PALACE

The abandoned cloisters of the Glaoui palace in Fez seem to hold and magnify the ancient city's enchanted quality like a prism. Brilliantly decorated in high Andalusian style, the sprawling palace of a hundred rooms arrayed around a dozen courtyards lies slowly fading beneath the African sun. Forsaken a scant half century ago by Thami El Glaoui, lord of the Atlas and pasha of Marrakech, when he fell from political grace, the palace feels as though it has been empty for centuries, inhabited only by ghosts and memories of long-dead residents. In reality, it is little more than a century old and its courts are not completely abandoned, thanks to the stewardship of Abdelkhalek Boukhars, the grandson of the pasha's retainer, who lives there with his extended family. ∽ Abdelkhalek was born and raised in the palace and his ancestors lie in a cemetery on its grounds. His family lives in the rooms surrounding one courtyard, hanging laundry from the colorfully painted balconies and curing strips of beef—a Fez delicacy—on wires suspended between *zellij* columns. Each day he guards the palace from his perch on the doorstep of the

OPPOSITE: *The ingredients for afternoon tea, Fez-style, are set upon a low tray. Essentials include bunches of fresh mint leaves, glossy pellets of Chinese gunpowder tea, and large lumps of sugar.*

155

ABOVE: *The polychrome wood doors and shutters throughout the palace reveal an unusually wide range of styles; this gold and lavender floral scheme is rare.*

OPPOSITE: *The steward, Abdelkhalek Boukhars, strides beneath the monumental arcade.*

primary entrance near the Bab Ziat, a gate opening into a neighborhood studded with derelict nineteenth-century palaces that attest to Fez's heyday of wealth and political power. Periodically, he tours the palace's courtyards and gardens accompanied by his German shepherd, Olga, to ensure that vandals have not ventured in to steal the valuable painted doors and shutters.

Carrying a large clasp of keys in the pocket of his *djellebah,* the keeper of the palace moves through its complicated matrix of halls and rooms with ease that comes from a lifetime of familiarity. Heaps of brocade pillows carefully zipped into muslin slipcovers lie piled in the corners of elaborately decorated salons. Heavy metal pots rust in the spacious kitchen where a giant stove capable of producing food for a feast stretches across an entire wall. Venetian glass mirrors decorated with delicately painted flowers and vines infinitely reflect each other's image across an empty room once filled with a pasha's harem.

When asked to host a traditional Moroccan tea in a palace courtyard, Abdelkhalek leaped at the opportunity to demonstrate the lavish hospitality for which Moroccans are famed. With the help of two friends—Mohammed Bouftila, a Muslim tour guide and historian with Spanish antecedents, and Ben Jelloun, a Jewish antiques dealer and actor (everyone seems to have two job descriptions in Fez, including Abdelkhalek, who is a respected artist), he assembled a fairy-tale party.

Moroccans love to drink tea, and the infusions they prepare vary widely. By far the most popular is mint tea, a tingling concoction of fresh mint, gunpowder tea (a Chinese green tea), and plenty of sugar. Lemon verbena is another popular infusion, but a favorite among the Fassi is absinthe tea brewed from the fresh herb that flavors the famously intoxicating liquor. Absinthe tea is particularly popular in the winter, when its blood-warming properties are most appreciated. For his tea party, Abdelkhalek assembled several herbs in order to provide a sampling of infusions.

Because the Fassi are famous for their cookies, Mohammed, or Momo, as friends call him, brought two boxes layered with freshly baked cookies, some crumbly with crushed nuts and powdered sugar and others sticky with honey glaze.

He also offered nougat, a chewy candy in pastel shades made from egg whites and sugar and flavored with fruit and nut extracts.

Ben arrived with a cart filled with antique serving dishes from his shop, L'Art Islamique: traditional Moroccan plates and bowls glazed in blues and yellows that reflect the colors of the palace's *zellij*, black and silver metal pitchers from the Rif Mountains, and wooden serving dishes emblazoned with silver Stars of David. Tucked beneath his arm were bags of fresh dates and almonds, ubiquitous snacks enjoyed throughout Morocco and the Middle East.

Abdelkhalek rifled through the rooms of the palace, discovering a crocheted lace tablecloth, embroidered napkins, and gilt-rimmed glasses. By midafternoon, tea was served beneath the window of a salon opening off the harem courtyard. Brightly painted shutters fanned open like butterfly wings to reveal a green and lavender scheme of floral medallions. A wrought iron window screen, its metal painted white, assumed the delicacy of Belgian lace. Above the window, a demilune panel of painted wood fringed by a border of carved plaster spread out like a peacock's tail.

At the end of this interlude celebrating the more feminine side of Moroccan style, Abdelkhalek and his friends revealed a surprise. In the grand courtyard of the palace, a massive space surrounded by a majestic arcade of horseshoe arches, they had prepared another meal. Foregoing tablecloths and cutlery, they served a rustic dinner of Fez's famous pigeon pie accompanied by flatbread and vegetable salads. Sitting on leather cushions and a marble step leading into the grand salon where Thami El Glaoui once entertained Winston Churchill, the men pinched off bites of the savory pastry and washed them down with hot mint tea. While Abdelkhalek regaled the company with tales of the celebrations that once took place in the pasha's palace, the sounds of this small gathering of friends echoed through the cavernous court like the voices of long-departed revelers.

OPPOSITE (LEFT): *The crocheted lace cloth and linen napkins embroidered with point de Fez, reveal the combined influences of Western and Eastern styles upon Fassi design.*

OPPOSITE (RIGHT): *The well-preserved architecture of the palace includes fine examples of wet-carved plaster borders that still retain their original paint.*

Moroccan Mint Tea
(Makes 6 cups)

2 teaspoons Chinese gunpowder tea
20 sprigs of fresh mint
1/2 cup sugar

Bring a kettle of water to a boil. Place the tea and 14 sprigs of the mint into a teapot that holds 6 cups of water. Fill the pot with boiling water and stir in the sugar. Cover and steep for 4 minutes. Place 1 sprig of mint in each tea glass and pour the hot tea over the mint and serve.

B'stila (Mock Pigeon Pie)

(Makes one 10-inch round pie)

In this recipe, free-range chicken is substituted for the pigeon traditionally used in Morocco.

3 tablespoons vegetable oil

1 large onion, finely chopped

3 garlic cloves, minced

1/2 cup finely chopped flat-leaf parsley

1/4 cup finely chopped cilantro

1/4 teaspoon turmeric

10 threads saffron, toasted and crushed

1 teaspoon ground ginger

2 1/4 teaspoons ground cinnamon

1 cup water

3 pounds boneless, skinless free-range chicken pieces
(half breasts, half thighs)

1 teaspoon salt

1/2 teaspoon freshly ground black pepper

1 1/3 cup confectioners' sugar

3 large eggs, beaten

1 cup (2 sticks), plus 1 tablespoon butter

1/2 cup whole blanched almonds

1 package 14 x 18 inch sheets phyllo dough, thawed

1 cup unsalted butter, melted, for brushing (2 sticks)

Ground cinnamon and confectioners' sugar for garnish

Preheat the oven to 450 degrees F.

Heat the oil in a deep skillet or Dutch oven over medium heat. Add the onion and garlic, and cook until translucent but not browned. Add the parsley, cilantro, turmeric, saffron, ginger, 1 1/4 teaspoons cinnamon, and water. Cook for 1 minute, stirring to mix. Add the chicken, cover, and cook over medium heat for 25 minutes or until the chicken is tender. Remove the chicken from the pan and let cool. Reduce the pan juices to 1 cup. Add the salt, pepper, and 2/3 cup sugar to the pan juices, and continue cooking over medium heat. Add the eggs and stir until the mixture forms a wet scrambled consistency. Remove from heat. Shred the chicken, adding it to the egg mixture.

Melt 1 tablespoon of butter in a skillet. Add the almonds and toast until golden. Place the almonds in a food processor with the remaining sugar and cinnamon and chop coarsely.

Butter a large baking sheet with raised edges. Stack 3 layers of phyllo in the center of the sheet, brushing each layer with butter. Sprinkle with half the almond mixture. Layer 3 more sheets of buttered phyllo sheets at a 90 degree angle to the first stack. Spread the chicken mixture in a 10-inch wide circle in the middle of the phyllo. Fold the edges of the phyllo over the chicken mixture. Stack 3 more buttered phyllo sheets over the chicken. Sprinkle with the remaining almond mixture. Add 3 more buttered phyllo sheets at a 90 degree angle. Tuck the edges of the phyllo underneath the pie to create a neat, tight circle. Brush with butter.

Bake for 20 to 25 minutes, until golden brown. Dust evenly with confectioners' sugar and decorate with cinnamon in a pattern of intersecting lines. Serve hot or warm.

Tower of Sand

MINISTERO DEL GUSTO

Diffuse golden light glows against rough walls and columns made of mud and sand. Flowing water sings with the gentle insistence of an underground stream opening suddenly into the echoing volume of a stone cave. Bones hang on walls inscribed with pictograms of fish, birds, bicycles, mandala, and five-pointed stars. Lamps made from dried agave flowers and horns of twisted parchment radiate faint light from corners. ∼ Were it not for clusters of mod furniture from the 1960s and 1970s, this elemental dwelling might easily be confused with the home of ancient man. Although inspired by the simple huts of Africa's earliest inhabitants, the structure is, in fact, the modern-day atelier of expatriate Italian designers Alessandra Lippini and Fabrizio Bizzarri. Credit for the studio's unusual design also belongs to Lippini's husband, photographer and former architect Nadir Naldi. ∼ Morocco is a crossroads for many ancient cultures: Africa, the Middle East, the Roman Empire, and Andalusian Spain, to name a few. As such, it is one of the most fertile places

OPPOSITE: *While Andalusian-style houses typically feature* zellij *and wet-carved plaster, at Ministero del Gusto the point of reference is the earthier architecture of Mali, translated with eccentric flair by a trio of Italian designers.*

162

OPPOSITE: *The roof terrace combines elements of the Dogon architecture of Mali and the adobe architecture of New Mexico.*

ABOVE: *Inspiration for the windows came from Gaudí's architecture; for the rope railing, from sailboats; and for the horn-shaped light fixture, from Fortuny.*

to tap into the archetypal signs and symbols of a global collective unconscious. It is this unbroken connection with a rich and ancient past that attracted Lippini and Bizzarri to live and work in Marrakech.

"Why do I live here?" Bizzarri muses. "The spirit of the place, the earth, the elemental quality, the material, the craftsmen—these are things I connect with." Lippini, who moved to Marrakech after working there on a fashion shoot with her husband eleven years ago, also waxes eloquently on the subject. "The Oriental atmosphere of the place captured my imagination," she recalls. "Then, there weren't as many Westerners living here, and you could become completely lost in a truly amazing place."

By allowing themselves to dream, unfettered by traditional ideas about how buildings should be constructed, how rooms should be decorated, how art and furniture should look, they created a unique environment for working and living which they named Ministero del Gusto, or the Ministry of Taste. The concept for the atelier began in Lippini's mind's eye as a tower of sand. Inspired by the Dogon architecture of Mali, Lippini, Bizzarri, and Naldi began to reconstruct a dilapidated dwelling in the Marrakech medina, covering its walls with a mixture of sand, straw, clay, and oxide paint and studding them with rough sticks reminiscent of the wooden supports used in Mali's sand houses.

Although neither Lippini nor Bizzarri have actually been to Central Africa, they did not consider this to be a disadvantage in absorbing its style lessons. The two studied photographs of the area's architecture, including a mud-walled room covered with irregularly spaced niches. They borrowed this idea, sculpting walls and ceilings into honeycomb shapes painted shades of red, lavender, ochre, and brown.

On a large interior wall, Lippini and Bizzarri fulfilled another shared vision: "We wanted to make a wall covered with all the graffiti we've had in our minds since childhood," Bizzarri explains. In addition to Western sources of graffiti, they also drew inspiration from the commercial signage of African villages, where the fishmonger scribbles a fish on his wall; the butcher, a chicken; the mechanic, a bicycle. "We even included the Mercedes-Benz symbol," Bizzarri concludes. "Why not? The whole philosophy of this place is 'Why not try this, why not try that?'"

BELOW: Caveman style collides with a slyly surrealist aesthetic in this second floor nook.

Opposite the graffiti wall is a two-story waterfall that glides down a gleaming *tadlekt* surface into a wide gray pool. Above the pool, a tower rises higher than the roofline to accommodate clerestory windows that are the source of the atelier's soft light. Seen from the roof, this structure resembles an adobe dwelling from New Mexico—another place Lippini has visited and admired. "If you reflect a little, you'll see there is a common line linking New Mexico and Mexico, India, and Africa," Bizzarri comments. "Maybe it's the latitude, or the heat, or the materials."

Celebrating the aesthetic of bricolage, which calls for the creative reuse of whatever materials (or signs and symbols) are at hand, Lippini and Bizzarri's free-wheeling approach to design is ruled only by their instincts and their dreams. As a result, they have succeeded in rewriting, or even unwriting, the rules of taste to create a uniquely personal, unpredictable, and inimitable ministry of taste. "We love to come to work every morning," exclaims Lippini. "It is so beautiful here."

OPPOSITE (LEFT): Bizzarri and Lippini created a graffiti wall inscribed with a free-ranging array of shapes and symbols.

OPPOSITE (RIGHT): Horn bracelets decorate columns, evoking images of African women bedecked for tribal celebrations.

Maghreb Mania

MOMO RESTAURANT FAMILIAL

From gentle dreams to fevered hallucinations, the full spectrum of the North African fantasy is explored at Momo Restaurant Familial, Kemia Bar, and Mô Tea Room on London's Heddon Street. All three are creations of Mourad Mazouz, better known as Momo to his friends, clients, and the international press, all of whom seem entranced by the fusion fantasies he invokes through decor, cuisine, and music. ∽ Born in Algeria but a citizen of the world, Momo spent his early twenties traveling the globe, with stints in the Far and Middle East, New York, Los Angeles, and Paris. In Egypt, he became intrigued with the country's mud architecture—both traditional houses built from earth and new designs by one of the country's most important contemporary architects, Hassan Fathy. In New York, he fell in love with the city's vibrant youth culture and nightclub scene. After working for high-end restaurants in New York, Aspen, and Hawaii, he decided it was time to open his own restaurant. Moving to Paris in his midtwenties, he opened an intimate bistro called Au Bascou that went on to win the prestigious Bistro of the Year Award.

OPPOSITE: *At London's Momo Restaurant Familial and Mô Tea Room, all the accoutrements of a sybaritic Moroccan setting—a silver lmrach for dispensing droplets of orange flower water, heady incense, flickering candlelight, and a scattering of fragrant rose petals—are at hand.*

ABOVE AND OPPOSITE:
Whether delivering
recipes and decorative
accessories saturated with
bright color and flavor or
concocting a sophisticated
Orientalist setting, Momo
is equally in tune with his
North African roots and
the demands of his trend-
savvy international
clientele.

"During the years I lived in America, I didn't think much about my own native culture," he recalls. "But my roots began to call me back when I was living in Paris." So Momo decided to open a restaurant serving Algerian and Moroccan cuisine called 404. Momo made it his business to prove that his culture could be cool and funky. While he chose a sixteenth-century stone house that reminded him of the stone architecture of North Africa's Berbers for the site of the restaurant, he decorated it in a minimalist Arabic style that quickly won the approval of a chic Parisian clientele.

In 1997, Momo brought that same combination of North African sensuality and New World cool to London with Momo Restaurant Familial. While the decor at Momo draws more on the decorative traditions of North Africa than that of 404, with walls of roughly applied plaster and windows screened with handmade *mousharabiya*, the food, music, and atmosphere reveals its owner's iconoclastic edge. During the daytime, a mood of sophisticated elegance pervades the restaurant, where light filters in through intricate wood screens and bounces off creamy plaster. A prix-fixe lunch features colorful, bright tasting dishes that combine typical Maghreb ingredients in unexpected combinations.

Momo is quick to point out that the cuisines of Tunisia, Algeria, and Morocco integrate a wide range of influences from the Middle East and the Mediterranean with a twentieth-century infiltration of French technique. Working with his Algerian chef, Mohamed Ourad, Momo creates an ever-changing repertoire of recipes for his restaurant that reveals an inventive approach to mixing and matching these diverse influences. Pesto couscous combines that most North African of staples with pure Italian flavors to create a delightfully surprising (and beautiful) green timbale surrounded by pan-fried scallops and shrimp and finished with a red pepper coulis. A saddle of lamb stuffed with wild mushrooms and wrapped in phyllo dough recalls pastry-encased French preparations, but the addition of preserved lemons and Ras el Hanout (a Moroccan spice mixture including turmeric, ginger, and mace) contributes distinct North African notes.

BELOW: *Moroccan-style wood chairs and brass tray-topped tables spill onto the sidewalk at Mô Tea Room, inviting passers-by to indulge in a pot of freshly steeped mint tea.*

The menu also includes more traditional Moroccan fare, including *harira* (a spicy vegetable soup) and *méchoui* (roasted lamb served on festival occasions) so that diners can explore the roots of North African cuisine. Other offerings such as pan-fried duckling with a shallot tart tatin are unrecognizable as Maghreb concoctions. And hybridized dishes like a dessert of Berber pancakes (crêpelike disks) layered in a mille-feuille with fresh fruit and strawberry coulis perfectly marry traditional and contemporary cuisine from Morocco and France.

This kaleidoscopic approach to taste is reflected in the surroundings, especially at night, when a pulsing sound track of world music compiled by Momo throbs through the restaurant's two floors. Flickering lanterns illuminate the dining room, which is divided into two areas including a raised *salon marocain*. But the most festive area is the members-only Kemia Bar in the basement, which glows with warm light and conviviality late into the evening. Here, in a room that was once a World War II bomb shelter, Momo has created an Orientalist pleasure dome by covering the ceiling with rough wooden beams and amber *tadlekt* and hanging vintage panels from a sheik's tent on the walls.

Recently, Momo extended his talents to create the Mô Tea Room, which opened next door to Momo Restaurant Familial in late 1999. Inspired by the tea shops found on every main street in North Africa, this property offers light lunch dishes and a selection of Arabic teas and pastries throughout the day. For those who wish to create their own *salons marocains* back home, Mô Tea Room is also a bijou bazaar featuring a selection of Islamic antiques and contemporary North African designs for purchase.

Momo's sense of excitement about his native culture and its potential to be revisited and reinvented is unbounded. Those who wish to tap into this inspired approach to fusing the exotic with the familiar, the ancient with the new, can do so by visiting Momo's and Mô Tea Room, listening to the global music mix of his compilations, *Arabesque* and *Africanesque,* and cooking the recipes he recently shared in *The Momo Cookbook.* If there is any lesson to be learned from Momo's approach to North African culture, it is that this is a vibrant, relevant tradition open to interpretation and accessible to all.

LEFT: *Contemporary and antique decorative objects from North Africa, Egypt, Syria, and Iran on sale at Mô Tea Room put the ingredients of the Orientalist fantasy within reach of Momo's clientele.*

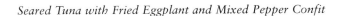

Halve the eggplants lengthwise and scoop out some of the flesh with a spoon. Place the eggplant halves on a plate and sprinkle them evenly with 1 tablespoon of sea salt. Cover with plastic wrap and chill for 2 hours.

Cut the peppers into ½-inch wide strips. In a frying pan over medium heat, heat 2 tablespoons of olive oil with the garlic, 1 teaspoon thyme, and 1 teaspoon sea salt. After 1 minute, add the peppers and reduce heat to low. Cook the peppers until soft, about 10 minutes. Remove from the oil to cool.

Put the balsamic vinegar in a small saucepan and cook over medium-high heat until reduced by half. Stir in the honey.

Remove the eggplants from the refrigerator, rinse under cold water, and dry. In a frying pan over medium-high heat, heat the vegetable oil. When hot, fry the eggplants, turning once, until tender.

Sprinkle 1 teaspoon thyme, 1 teaspoon paprika, and 1 teaspoon sea salt on a board. Roll the tuna in this mixture. In a frying pan over high heat, heat the remaining 2 tablespoons of olive oil. When the oil is hot, sear the tuna on all sides, cooking 3 to 4 minutes for rare tuna. Remove the tuna from the heat to a clean cutting board. Slice thinly, on the diagonal.

To serve, place one eggplant half filled with mixed pepper confit on each plate. Sprinkle with chopped cilantro and minced hot pepper. Arrange tuna slices next to the vegetables. Drizzle with vinegar reduction.

Seared Tuna with Fried Eggplant and Mixed Pepper Confit

(Serves 6 as an appetizer)

3 small eggplants, peeled, stem on

2 teaspoons plus 1 tablespoon sea salt

6 mixed bell peppers (red, yellow, green), seeded

4 tablespoons olive oil

2 cloves garlic, minced

2 teaspoons dried thyme

¼ cup balsamic vinegar

1 tablespoon honey

2 tablespoons vegetable oil

1 pound tuna

1 teaspoon paprika

2 tablespoons fresh cilantro, finely chopped

1 small hot pepper, minced (optional)

Salt and pepper to taste

Pesto Couscous with Pan-Fried Scallops and Rock Shrimp with a Red Pepper Coulis

(Serves 6)

1 package (10 ounces) instant couscous

2 red bell peppers

7 tablespoons olive oil

4 garlic cloves, chopped

4 branches fresh thyme (or 1 teaspoon dried thyme)

Salt and freshly ground black pepper to taste

1 bunch fresh basil

40 pine nuts

1 cup finely grated Parmesan cheese

24 sea scallops

¹/₂ cup finely chopped cilantro leaves

1¹/₂ teaspoon sweet paprika

18 rock shrimp, unpeeled, head on

Prepare the couscous according to the package directions and keep warm in a double boiler.

Cut the peppers into 2-inch pieces. Heat 2 tablespoons of the oil in a frying pan over medium heat. Add half of the chopped garlic and all the peppers and cook for about 7 minutes, until the peppers are soft. Add the leaves from the thyme branches, and the salt and pepper. Cook over low heat for a half hour. Puree the mixture and keep warm.

Remove the basil leaves from the stems and chop them. In a large mortar bowl, combine the basil, remaining garlic, pine nuts, 3 tablespoons olive oil, Parmesan cheese, and salt and pepper. Pound the ingredients with a pestle to form a paste.

Put 2 tablespoons of olive oil in a wide sauté pan over medium-high heat. Dredge the scallops in a mixture of chopped cilantro, paprika, and salt and pepper to taste. When the oil is hot, put the scallops in the pan and cook on each side for 1 minute. Remove the scallops from the pan. Sprinkle salt and pepper on the shrimp. Place them in the hot oil, cooking on each side for 1 minute.

In a bowl, mix the warm couscous well with the pesto. Place timbales of pesto couscous on each plate. Spoon the pepper coulis around the timbale. Arrange the shrimp and scallops around the couscous.

Pesto Couscous with Pan-Fried Scallops and Rock Shrimp

THE MEDINAS OF MOROCCO BUSTLE WITH THRONGS OF

people, animals, and vehicles by day, but at night they become lonely labyrinths. Deeply shaded tunnels and doors hung with knockers in the shape of human hands lend the stone and stucco mazes an eerie mood. A dreamy aura settles over the old cities, collecting in the private courtyards and thick-walled rooms of houses where it lingers on in daylight like a collective reverie. This is the mood of Moroccan repose, which offers respite from frenetic city street life and access to waking dreams.

Morocco's architecture nearly always turns a blank wall to the street, folding in around a series of enclosed spaces: courtyards, arcades, and rooms with windows opening only along interior walls. In the countryside, farmhouses are frequently enclosed by walls, and along the valleys of the Atlas Mountains, entire walled villages called *ksour* turn in upon themselves. These structures form oases of quiet and beauty amid the often harsh surroundings of Morocco's urban and rural settings.

In traditional Andalusian-style courtyards, precious shade, refreshing fountains, and scented trees and flowers inspire serenity despite the bright and busy patterns of *zellij* that cover walls and columns. In recent years, homeowners, hoteliers, and designers have recognized the power of less highly charged settings to invoke a sense of calm. By reducing color to a single tone or using a natural palette of matte white plaster, sun-paled cedar, and unglazed tile they soothe the senses. These modern-day practitioners of peacefulness remind us that the essence of Moroccan style is neither strong color nor intense surface decoration but rather a balance between the embellished and the unadorned, excess and restraint, delirium and repose.

Riad Retreat

LUNCHEON AT RYAD TAMSNA

I t is easy to become overwhelmed by the Marrakech medina's tangled maze of streets. Disorientation is so common that out-of-town visitors rarely have a clear sense of where they are and whether they will make it to their desired destination until quite suddenly an intricately carved door with a familiar address appears before them, reassuring them that they have, indeed, arrived. ∽ Morocco's traditional *riad* architecture creates a perfect antidote to the hubbub of the medina's streets. The outer door opens into a small hallway—a decompression chamber that invites those who enter to sink into its quiet, cool embrace. On the far side of this entrance area lies a courtyard filled with gently rustling greenery and burbling fountains. At Ryad Tamsna, Meryanne Loum-Martin began with just such a gracious courtyard dwelling to which she added her own air of simple elegance to create a paradise of repose. ∽ A boutique for decorative accessories for the home, bath, and body, an art gallery, and a restaurant, Ryad Tamsna serves as a showcase for Loum-Martin's sophisticated approach to design, cuisine,

OPPOSITE: *A neutral palette prevails in Ryad Tamsna's two-story arcade, celebrating the natural colors of limestone plaster, carved cedar, and burnished metal.*

RIGHT: *The rooms and arcades surrounding the courtyard provide exhibition space for contemporary artisans, designers, and artists, including Moroccan painter Rita Alaoui, whose work is shown here.*

and the art of living. "I always have to fight against the temptation to get too elaborate or too ornate," she claims. Yet little evidence of this battle shows through her final design, which celebrates form, color, texture, and volume with uncluttered grace.

The palette of the *riad*'s courtyard is taken from the natural building materials: plaster the color of sand and earth, sun-bleached cedar doors, and the dark calligraphy of wrought-iron balconies. Against this neutral backdrop, the sunset shades of hand-woven textiles create welcome oases of color. Kilim rugs with stripes of orange and red, pillows upholstered in rust-red fabric woven in Senegal, and throws of heavy cotton duck finished with strips from vintage carpets brighten the space.

Like the architecture that surrounds it, the furniture is simple and monumental. In one corner of the courtyard, oversized chairs and a coffee table of metal burnished to resemble bronze create a comfortable seating area. Designed by Loum-Martin, the furniture is pierced with geometric patterns found frequently in Moroccan design, but the squared-off shapes are more reminiscent of the art deco furnishings of the French Protectorate. Candelabra pairing heavy columns of metal crowned with curving animal horns provide hints of both contemporary Western style and exotic African forms.

Visitors to the *riad* can enjoy a moment of repose in the courtyard before exploring rooms filled with art, textiles, metal crafts, and jewelry, or they can take a seat at one of the tables and enjoy lunch or dinner. The uniformed servers detail the day's offerings, describing menus that combine elements of French, Mediterranean, Middle Eastern, and North African cuisine in deceptively simple preparations.

One of Loum-Martin's favorite menus reflects the toned-down approach she brings to fusion. This luncheon commences with a Mediterranean variation on the *briouat*—a traditional Moroccan savory wrapped in paper-thin sheets of pastry called *warqa* (which means "leaf"). For her version, Loum-Martin uses phyllo to encase a mixture of sun-dried tomatoes and goat cheese. For the main course, she garnishes chicken breasts with a tingling ginger cherry sauce to create a truly international alchemy. Served with very French vegetable purees of carrots and fennel,

ABOVE: *Despite the contemporary nature of the art, design, and cuisine at Ryad Tamsna, the sensual traditions of Moroccan living are also observed, including the daily floating of fresh roses in the courtyard fountain.*

the entrée defies geographic classification. The dessert that follows—a poached pear drizzled with a honey-cinnamon sauce—is an equally successful union of culinary traditions.

While fusion cuisine and decor can often slide into cacophony, with too many bright colors, flavors, and textures, Loum-Martin manages to create serene marriages of ingredients from widely varied cultures. "The elements of a meal should not fight with each other for your attention," she explains. "Keep the flavors pure and just add a whisper of spice." When it comes to design, Loum-Martin has equally straightforward advice: "I like to keep to a single color family in each room. The drama can come from a sense of scale—something unexpectedly large, for instance—from the texture of natural materials, or from the shape of beautifully crafted objects. Let the language of the material or the artisan speak for itself."

A twenty-five-year resident of Paris and the offspring of the marriage of a Senegalese father and West Indian mother, Loum-Martin comes by her genius for fusion naturally. While not everyone has the benefit of her multicultural background, anyone can learn from Loum-Martin's example how to create subtle harmonies that delight the senses. Ryad Tamsna's cuisine and decor offer ideas about how to quietly invoke the sensual essence of Moroccan style in any setting.

ABOVE: *A new carved cedar door and bronze door knocker decorated with precise geometric patterns reveal the reverence with which contemporary craftsmen interpret traditional designs.*

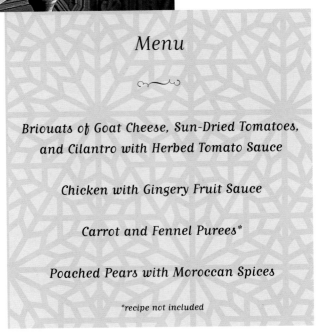

Menu

Briouats of Goat Cheese, Sun-Dried Tomatoes, and Cilantro with Herbed Tomato Sauce

Chicken with Gingery Fruit Sauce

Carrot and Fennel Purees*

Poached Pears with Moroccan Spices

*recipe not included

Briouats of Goat Cheese, Sun-Dried Tomatoes, and Cilantro
(Makes 24)

12 ounces soft, mild goat cheese, at room temperature

2 tablespoons sour cream

$3^{1}/_{2}$ tablespoons chopped cilantro

3 sun-dried tomatoes in oil, drained and chopped

Salt and freshly ground black pepper to taste

1 package 14 x 18 inch sheets phyllo dough, thawed

Olive oil for brushing

Sesame seeds for sprinkling

Preheat the oven to 375 degrees F.

Place the goat cheese and sour cream in the bowl of a food processor and blend until smooth. Add the cilantro, sun-dried tomatoes, and salt and pepper. Pulse until well blended. Place one sheet of phyllo pastry on a dry work surface (keeping the remaining phyllo sheets covered with a damp towel or plastic wrap). Brush the sheet with oil and using a sharp knife cut it into strips that are approximately 4 inches wide and 14 inches long. Put a heaping teaspoon of the filling at the top right corner of each strip. Fold the corner covered with the filling down to make a triangle. Continue folding the triangle down the length of the strip to make a packet. Brush the finished packet with oil. Repeat these steps until all the filling has been used. The *briouats* can be baked at once, kept cov-ered with plastic wrap in the refrigerator for 24 hours, or frozen for up to two weeks.

Bring the *briouats* to room temperature, if refrigerated or frozen. Lightly brush a baking sheet with the oil. Sprinkle the *briouats* with sesame seeds and bake for 20 minutes or until crisp and golden. Serve hot with Herbed Tomato Sauce (recipe follows) on the side.

Briouats with Herbed Tomato Sauce

183

Herbed Tomato Sauce

(Makes 1¹/₂ cups)

1 tablespoon olive oil
1 large onion, minced
3 large tomatoes, peeled, seeded, and chopped
1 serrano pepper, seeded and minced (optional)
¹/₄ teaspoon salt
Freshly ground black pepper to taste
¹/₂ cup chopped cilantro leaves

Heat the oil in a large sauté pan over medium heat. Add the onion and cook until translucent. Add the tomatoes and the serrano pepper and continue cooking over medium heat until the tomatoes break down and form a sauce. Add salt and pepper. Serve hot, garnished with cilantro.

Chicken with Gingery Fruit Sauce

(Serves 4)

4 skinless, boneless chicken breast halves
1 clove garlic, crushed
2¹/₂ tablespoons grated peeled fresh ginger
Salt and freshly ground black pepper to taste
2 tablespoons olive oil
2 onions, minced
Gingery Fruit Sauce (recipe follows)
Fresh cilantro leaves, chopped, for garnish

In a large glass bowl, toss the chicken breasts with the garlic, ginger, and salt and pepper. Cover with plastic wrap and marinate in the refrigerator for at least 30 minutes and up to 3 hours. When the chicken has finished marinating, heat the oil in a deep nonstick skillet or Dutch oven large enough to hold all the pieces in one layer. Remove the chicken breasts from the marinade, reserving marinade, and brown them evenly over medium-high heat.

Remove the browned chicken from the oil and place it in a clean large bowl. Add the chopped onions and reserved marinade to the pan and cook until the onions are translucent. Return the chicken to the pan along with any juices that have accumulated in the bowl. Cover and cook gently over low to medium heat for 30 minutes or until the chicken is tender and cooked through. Add a few tablespoons of water as needed to keep the chicken from drying out and sticking to the pan while cooking.

To serve, arrange the chicken on a plate and drizzle with Gingery Fruit Sauce (recipe follows). Sprinkle chopped cilantro over the plate. Serve pan juices in a bowl on the side. Basmati rice is a nice, but optional, addition to this main course.

Gingery Fruit Sauce

(Makes about 1¹/₂ cups)

¹/₂ tablespoon olive oil
2 small onions, minced

2 tablespoons grated peeled fresh ginger

1 jar (8 ounces) high-quality cherry
or blackberry preserves

Heat the oil in a medium saucepan over medium-high heat. When hot, add the onions and ginger. Cook gently until the onions become translucent but not brown. Add the fruit preserves and bring to a boil. Remove from heat immediately.

Poached Pears with Moroccan Spices
(Serves 4)

4 cups cold water

4 pears, not too ripe

5 tablespoons fresh lemon juice

³/₄ cup sugar

8 cloves

1 cinnamon stick (about 2 inches long)

¹/₂ cup honey

³/₄ teaspoon ground cinnamon

Slivered almonds for garnish

Pour 2 cups of the water and 1 tablespoon of the lemon juice in a medium bowl. Carefully peel the pears, remove the core using a coring tool, and cut off the narrow pointed end of the pear. Place the pears in the acidulated water to keep from discoloring.

In a saucepan large enough to hold all the

pears, combine the remaining 2 cups water with 2 tablespoons of lemon juice, the sugar, 4 of the cloves, and the cinnamon stick. Bring to a boil over medium-high heat. Gently drop the pears into the poaching liquid and reduce the heat to medium-low, simmering and turning occasionally for 10 minutes or until the pears are just tender. Let the pears cool to room temperature in the syrup.

To make the honey sauce, heat the honey with the remaining tablespoon of lemon juice, 4 cloves, and the ground cinnamon. Remove the pears from the poaching liquid, place them in small bowls or plates, and stud them with almond slivers. Drizzle with the warm honey sauce.

Modern Moorish Revival

DAR ANDALUSIA

Surrounded by homes with emerald-green lawns and extroverted facades, Glen and Liv Ballard's Beverly Hills house is street-shy and mysterious. Hidden behind a tall wall and a succulent tangle of tropical plants, the house turns inward to embrace a series of airy rooms and intimate gardens. "It's like living inside a beautiful conch shell," says Glen, a songwriter and music producer who often fills the house with musicians and their melodies. The 1926 creation of Jazz Age master builder Roy Seldon Price, the house is built in an American hybrid style blending the low-slung silhouette of Mediterranean revival architecture with exotic flourishes of Moorish design. A romantic marriage of horseshoe and Romanesque arches, white stucco and rustic wood beams, and hand-painted Mexican tile—part Spanish, part Moorish, part Spanish colonial—it is nearly impossible to separate the different strands of cultural influence at work in the design. The house also defies chronological classification, with its combination of Old World materials within a modern context of simple lines and free-flowing spaces.

OPPOSITE: *The floor plan of this early twentieth-century Mediterranean revival house in Los Angeles, with rooms opening off a central hall, is Anglo-European, but the white plaster surfaces and tile details lend an Andalusian air.*

Textiles inspired by
Indian and Persian
designs, studded doors,
frames inlaid with
mother-of-pearl, and sinu-
ous wrought iron details
add highlights of color,
texture, and pattern to
the luminous white back-
drop of the architecture.

"It lives in a very modern way for a house built in 1926," Liv remarks. "We wanted to keep it spare, so in that way, the decor is very modern, too." Despite the fact that a major renovation was required to reverse the effects of age and water damage, the Ballards and their Los Angeles–based interior designer Annie Kelly agreed that they did not want to interfere with the original spirit of the house. Once they succeeded in repairing the damage, they set about highlighting the essential beauty of the house.

Wood floors were given a dark espresso stain, and plaster walls were covered with a fresh coat of white paint. "You don't want to rev up the color in these Spanish style houses," Annie comments. "You need a peaceful palette." Illuminated by natural light that flows in through plentiful windows, the white walls reveal the irregular contours of hand-shaped plaster. Deep arches, niches, and geometrically carved moldings frame doors and windows. Exposed wooden beams and whimsical details—a studded leather door, a stained glass window—add variety to the architecture.

In a small sitting room, Annie added her own touch of sensual whimsy with a poured concrete floor tinted deep pink and accented with a channel of red river rocks. Working with Los Angeles architect Michael McKeel, she also designed a secret room in the formerly unused basement: an intimate wine tasting room illuminated by a red Moroccan lamp.

In choosing furniture and decorative details for the house, the Ballards and their decorator opted for an eclectic approach, mixing spare contemporary pieces including a long, white Christian Liaigre sofa with more ornate elements such as ivory inlaid Syrian and Moroccan sofas and mirrors and Gothic chairs. The overall palette of the furnishings—white and cream accented with dark iron and wood—matches that of the house. "I never envisioned the house as a riot of color," explains Liv. Still, there is plenty of color in textiles that add warm notes of pattern and hue throughout the toned-down rooms.

In the library, two armchairs and a hassock are upholstered in a Robert Kime fabric embroidered with a sinuous design of vines and flowers reminiscent of Indian textiles. In the long living room, which doubles as a music room when

RIGHT: *The once water-logged basement was transformed into a wine cellar with a tasting room complete with Moroccan chairs designed during the French Protectorate.*

BELOW: *An eclectic collection of highly charged furniture including this Gothic-style bed with elaborately turned and carved posts and headboard make strong visual statements throughout the house.*

Glen's friends and clients visit, two scroll-back chairs are covered in aubergine cashmere with red-and-gold fringe. A large ottoman upholstered with a gorgeously faded antique silk Turkish rug adds a note of Middle Eastern opulence.

Nearly every room has one or more Moroccan details—a small octagonal table, a spiraling Fortuny lamp echoing the shape of traditional Moroccan skin lanterns, antique prints depicting colorful Moorish motifs. But other influences creep in as well—intensely colored Indian fabric adds highlights in the master bedroom suite, and Mexican and Peruvian art complement the Spanish colonial aspects of the building's design.

Annie's own designs of wrought iron and carved wood bring all the influences together. For the living room, she created a massive banquette with Moroccan-inspired cutouts along its base. In the main dining room, she designed a table with a scrolled iron base that repeats a griffin motif found in the house's original ironwork. In an enclosed patio opening off the living room, a new outdoor fireplace repeats the round forms of the house's arches and niches and provides welcome warmth when the weather turns cool. "The climate here is much like the desert climate in Spain and Morocco," Liv points out. "It's often chilly in the morning and the evening."

Neither the Ballards nor their decorator had ever been to Morocco when they began work on the house. Annie interpreted Moroccan style through the lens of the Mediterranean revival, creating her own concept of modern Moorish revival. Liv allowed herself to be guided by an intuitive understanding of a style she had encountered primarily through books. When the Ballards traveled to Marrakech following the completion of the house, Liv received affirmation that her intuitions were right in line with the reality of Morocco.

"When I was in the crowded, dusty *souks* in Marrakech, I turned a corner and suddenly found myself in the peaceful courtyard of a *riad*," she recalls. "Then I realized that *this* is the essence of Morocco: the secret, sensual surprise." When she returned to her own house, she saw it with fresh eyes. "There are these wide open, white Andalusian spaces, then you turn a corner, go down a narrow staircase, and find yourself in the secret rooms down there," she explains. "There is a sense in this house that something wonderful is hidden just around the corner."

ABOVE: *Dark furniture with white inlaid details complements the white stucco walls and espresso-stained wood floor of the living room.*

191

Understated Orientalism

RIYAD EL MEZOUAR

Jérôme Vermelin and Michel Durand-Meyrier are new Orientalists—contemporary French aesthetes drawn to Morocco by its ancient architecture and sensual way of life. Jérôme's ties to the East originate from early travels to China where his parents lived for many years and where he began collecting art and decorative objects. Michel's connections date to the last decades of the French Protectorate, when his great-uncle served as a high-ranking diplomat in Morocco. Despite the fact that the two men were well versed in the history of Orientalism—Jérôme as an architect, Michel as an artist, and both as collectors—neither had visited Morocco until eight years ago. ⌒〰 "It was spring. The gardens were green. It was a magical season for the city," recalls Jérôme. "I loved everything," Michel agrees. "The people, the monuments, the architecture, the sun, the landscape." The pair began making regular trips until they bought an eighteenth-century *riad* in the Marrakech medina three years ago and transformed it into Riyad El Mezouar, their primary home and a guesthouse. Combining their art and design backgrounds, Jérôme and Michel

OPPOSITE: *The fusion of French and Moroccan decorative arts, popular in the late nineteenth and early twentieth centuries, finds fresh expression in the hands of expatriate French designers Jérôme Vermelin and Michel Durand-Meyrier.*

renovated and decorated the house, developed a line of furniture, and launched an interior design firm called La Cour Des Myrtes (Myrtle Court).

When they acquired the house, once the home of the pasha of Marrakech's nephew, it had been poorly renovated in a tawdry interpretation of Andalusian style. The courtyard was covered in cheap, modern tile of blue and yellow, rooms had been subdivided into tiny chambers, an ancient staircase had been removed, and makeshift bathrooms and kitchens were scattered about. "It was horrible, really tasteless," Michel exclaims.

Michel and Jérôme stripped away all the modern materials and restored the rooms to their original proportions. They covered the walls with plain white plaster and removed layers of paint from the original iron balustrades. They added a pool lined with green tiles inspired by the color of antique roof tiles and surrounded it with flower beds filled with French, Spanish, and Moroccan plants. The end result is an elegantly restrained retreat that perfectly expresses the designers' twin passions for European refinement and Orientalist exoticism.

White walls enclose the courtyard with a graceful succession of arched openings. The arcade's reflection shimmers in the green pool, which is fed by a marble fountain afloat with rose petals. Ornately carved doors and shutters stripped down to pale natural cedar open into spare rooms bathed in diffuse sunlight. These rooms provide the ideal setting for Jérôme's and Michel's designs—furniture characterized by subtle drama, simple lines, and oblique cultural references.

A tall antique vase with a celadon glaze stands at one end of an open-air sitting room, and an iron secretary desk that invokes the geometric serenity of Ming dynasty furniture stands at the other. These flank an unadorned contemporary sofa and chair. On the floor, a Moroccan carpet woven in shades of oxblood and celadon recalls the palette of Chinese ceramics. On another of the *riad*'s colonnades, a similarly minimalist fusion scene is set. A classical urn salvaged from the renovated Mamounia Hotel stands beneath a cusped Moroccan arch. Beneath it sits a contemporary chaise longue, its spare lines and simple striped upholstery conjuring comparisons to Swedish design.

LEFT AND BELOW:
Whether decorating a corner of their riad or preparing a tea-time snack of oranges preserved in sugar syrup, the designers demonstrate their love for clean lines, pure shapes, and sophisticated color combinations.

More overt references to Swedish style can be found in a guest bedroom that easily blends an array of Eastern and Western influences. In one corner, an armchair with French eighteenth-century lines and a Swedish-style finish of gray glaze sits next to an octagonal table. Reminiscent of the little tables found in nearly every *salon marocain*, this design is simplified and finished with a pale glaze that is distinctly non-Moroccan. Standing nearby, a wooden console—European in form and Swedish in its matte gray finish—is clearly Moroccan in ornamentation, with a row of geometric cutouts running across its apron. Two Chinese jars atop the console add an Asian note, while a gilded footstool tucked beneath marries Directoire and Ming dynasty influences.

Only in the *grand salon*—a long, narrow room used for entertaining—do Michel and Jérôme surrender completely to the mode of Orientalist decadence. A long banquette clad in dark red fabric lines one wall. A Tibetan banner of maroon silk painted with golden clouds and landscape elements billows above the divan. Portraits of turbaned Turkish sultans hang on the walls, a Moroccan rug covers the floor, and an inlaid Syrian table adds yet another degree of opulent detail.

While at first glance this exotic room seems to be very Moroccan in character, it might also pass as the Parisian atelier of a nineteenth-century Orientalist painter returning home with souvenirs from his distant travels. The French, who after all invented chinoiserie, have long loved to surround themselves with objects that combine European and Oriental design. As the newest generation of French Orientalists, Jérôme and Michel are quick to point out that their style is as much European as it is Moroccan. "We were already 'fusion' before we came here," says Michel.

Enchanted Tower

RIAD KAISS

In the rooms and gardens of Riad Kaiss, expatriate French architect Christian Ferre explores the many modes of Moroccan style, from the highly charged to the elegantly minimal, the unabashedly romantic to the quietly serene. Despite this stylistic diversity, there is a unifying mood of repose that lingers throughout the 150-year-old *riad* like the scent of an elusive bloom. "I love the medina and the energy of the streets, but I also love to come into the *riad*, hear the birds, and feel the cool air of the courtyard," Ferre explains. "It is these contrasts that make the Moroccan experience so rich." Riad Kaiss, which serves both as Ferre's home and a popular guesthouse, is approached by a series of ever narrowing, winding footpaths that leave the busy streets and square of the medina behind as they lead guests to a large wooden door. On the far side of this door, the splashing of a courtyard fountain echoes throughout the labyrinth of rooms, terraces, and stairs. The constant rustling of tall cedars, green cascades of vines, and palm fronds soothes the spirit. And the surreal beauty of the architecture, with its spiraling staircases and undulating arches, creates a dreamy atmosphere.

OPPOSITE: *Just two stories above the busy streets of Marrakech, this secluded pavilion offers sanctuary from the dust and noise below. Decorative details including columns with elaborate capitals and a divan fashioned from* mousharabiya *create an exotic atmosphere.*

198

ABOVE: *The sound of the marble fountain splashing in the lushly planted courtyard fills the corridors and rooms of Riad Kaiss.*

RIGHT: *Ferre's architectural sensibilities find full expression in his private sitting room, where a fireplace with a tall, scalloped chimney dominates.*

200

The traditional architecture of the *riad*, with its polychrome wooden doors and ceilings and elaborate *zellij*, invited a conventional approach to Moroccan decor. Ferre followed this thread in the courtyard and a *salon marocain* decorated with Berber rugs, round brass tables, and low divans that invite guests to lounge in Oriental splendor. But when guests begin to explore the *riad*, opening doors and climbing staircases that wind through rose-colored walls, they begin to appreciate Ferre's versatility as an architect who is equally comfortable with traditional opulence and contemporary minimalism.

One door tucked into a corner of the courtyard opens into a narrow spiral staircase where striped green *tadlekt* walls wind upward like the central spine of a shell. Around another corner, stairs ascend straight to the sky, opening into a pavilion where walls of *mousharabiya* frame views of the courtyard below. The guest rooms vary widely in size, shape, and style. Some are utterly traditional, with ceilings of interwoven oleander branches and horseshoe arched windows, while others are quite contemporary, with pared-down furnishings and uniform color schemes.

The most minimalist guest room features off-white walls of plaster surmounted by a bright white

RIGHT: *A black-and-white frieze of Arabic text provides a strikingly graphic detail in this bedroom.*

201

frieze inscribed with black calligraphy. A simple pattern of black-and-white tile covers the floor and floor-to-ceiling curtains of white cotton flutter along one wall. French doors open onto a terrace that provides an ideal vantage point for enjoying the courtyard below. But guests versed in Arabic may prefer to stay inside and ponder the proverbs inscribed upon the walls: "A real man is the one who says, I am here to face my own problems and to make my own world." "No one ever receives all that he desires—the wind goes against all boats." "Fortune belongs to the one who has enough courage and ambition."

While this suite has the spiritual air of a sage's contemplation room, the most magical rooms of all belong to Ferre, whose rooftop retreat of twin pavilions surveys the sky and distant mountain peaks. Decorated in white, black, and blue, these rooms provide a serene retreat. The first, a private sitting room, is dominated by a fireplace of white plaster molded into sinuous curves and jutting angles. Ossified ostrich eggs provide white-on-white detail on the mantel. Shadow boxes filled with found objects hang on the walls, their gridlike patterns echoing the intersecting lines of the *zellij* floor.

Geometry also creates a sense of order and balance on the private terrace, where thin bands of blue-and-black *zellij* crisscross large squares of white tile. A second pavilion rises on the far side of the terrace to house the master bedroom—a light-filled suite with a soaring pyramidal roof. A large bed of iron and wicker nearly fills the room. Above it hangs a surrealist painting depicting the pages of a giant book held open by a gray plumed bird. The fantastic image captures the dreamlike quality of the room that floats above the city like an enchanted tower. "It is very pure up here," Ferre muses. "To wake up in the morning and see the sky, the trees . . . it is a wonderful thing."

A wall crowned with a typical Moroccan geometric motif separates Ferre's bedroom from a bath and dressing room area. The painting by Korean artist Ko Young Hoon captures the sense of serenity and other-worldliness that permeates this rooftop retreat.

Paradise Found

VILLA ARGANA

Villa Argana seems to exist in the middle of nowhere and no time—the perfect coordinates for experiencing total repose. While it might not be advisable to tackle the unpaved road leading to the villa in the dark, the most romantic hour to arrive at Argana is at dusk, when a path of twinkling lanterns lights the way through a rock garden to an inner courtyard. There, irregularly shaped windows framed by whitewashed stone are lit from within by tiny candles and the villa's hand-hewn architecture glimmers with an otherworldly charm. ⌒⌒ Villa Argana lies only a short drive from Essaouira—a seaside town with a busy port afloat with a colorful wooden fishing fleet. But its closest neighbors are herds of cows and goats, and the air is filled with the scent of wildflowers, the tinkling of cowbells, and the floating songs of birds. "My favorite thing about Villa Argana is the calm," confesses its owner, London-based musician Andy Gwatkin. "It is silent, but the silence holds sound."

OPPOSITE: *Heavy velvet-clad pillows and a wrought-iron chandelier provide notes of refined sensuality in this rustic, open-air dining area. A floor of river stones and swaying canopy of dried broom shift constantly underfoot and overhead.*

205

OPPOSITE: *A sheepskin rug softens the stone floor in the bathroom, where boulders from the nearby River Ksab form a bathtub (fed by solar-heated water) that overlooks a wildflower garden.*

OVERLEAF: *On cool nights, the wood-burning fireplace efficiently warms this low-ceilinged, thick-walled bedroom. In the morning, the rising sun pours through the small windows, illuminating the muslin bed-hangings and reflecting on the white-washed walls.*

Andy and his companion, London artist Micol Strauss, first came to Morocco twelve years ago, then returned after another six. They arrived in Agadir—a thoroughly modern seaside resort—and quickly moved on to Essaouira where they found the beauty and regional character they sought. When they decided to build a retreat for themselves that would also serve as a guesthouse for adventurous tourists, they settled on a piece of land in Ghazoua, a small village about ten kilometers outside of Essaouira.

"We discovered this place and were seduced by it," Andy recounts. "It's just so rooted." Falling beneath the spell of the Berber village, Andy and Micol began to design their retreat, employing the traditional building materials and forms used by the local people. For the main structure of the house, they chose the simple shape of Berber farmhouses—typically one-story complexes of rooms wrapped around a courtyard.

Because timber is scarce in the arid landscape, the area's principal building material is stone. With the help of local workers, Andy constructed the villa from rocks dug out of what is now the garden. They left the exterior walls a natural gray brown and whitewashed the interior spaces to create reflective surfaces that make the most of natural light and candle illumination. The ceilings are constructed from hand-hewn beams and branches of eucalyptus and sabra.

Loose river stones collected from the nearby River Ksab cover the floor. These stones shift and settle underfoot to create a richly textured floor that is softened with colorfully striped kilims and sheepskin rugs. Weighty velvet cushions, billowing cotton draperies, lace tablecloths, and roughly woven blankets provide more contrast in color and feel. Locally made pottery overflows with simple arrangements of wildflowers and handwrought iron sconces and candelabra hold plain white tapers. In the bathrooms, tubs fashioned from boulders give bathers the impression that they are soaking in a secluded spring.

With no electricity, the villa is designed to function well within the natural environment. Low-ceilinged rooms with stone walls hold heat produced by wood-burning fireplaces at night and offer a cool retreat during hot afternoons. Small windows emit bright light that bounces off white walls. In the morning, the sunlight pours through these apertures, illuminating gossamer canopies of muslin and bamboo and making them glow like sails on ghostly ships.

The windows frame views of the surrounding garden where spiky aloe plants, ethereal yellow mimosa trees, and star-faced daisies grow in natural profusion. Inside the courtyard, terra-cotta containers filled with cactuses ornament a Romanesque arcade of stucco columns crowned by rough stone capitals. An enthusiast of ancient architecture, Andy enjoyed reinventing classic forms with the raw materials at hand. "We discovered that we could make a Gothic pointed arch by putting two long stones together," he explains.

In keeping with the design of ancient Roman dwellings, where an outdoor dining area was often tucked into a shaded corner of the courtyard, Villa Argana has a grottolike area for alfresco meals. A semi-circular bench softened by rose-tinted velvet pillows hugs a rough stone wall. Tassels of dried broom hang from a trellis that shades the table in daytime. A wrought-iron chandelier illumines the bower at night. Here, guests enjoy breakfasts of just-baked flatbreads served with local honey or dinners of Atlantic fish caught by Essaouira's fishermen.

After meals, the rooftop terrace offers a place to sit and survey the surrounding countryside that has changed little over the last millennium or two. According to Andy, the best time to enjoy the terrace is at night, when he likes to lie on one of the sheepskin rugs and count the countless stars. "I can lie here for hours and look at the sky," Andy sighs. "The hours just slip by. Everything is right."

Glossary ⁓

Note: Many of the following terms are transliterated from the Arabic alphabet into the Roman alphabet. Roman alphabet spellings of Arabic terms are based on phonetics and vary widely.

bassin: a large, flat manmade pool of water incorporated in a landscape design, often as a reflecting element for the surrounding features.

Berber: African people who have lived in the deserts and mountains of Morocco since prehistoric times and whose descendants formed several powerful dynasties.

briouat: a Moroccan savory usually made of meat- or cheese-based filling wrapped in paper-thin sheets of pastry called *warqa* (which means "leaf").

b'stila: a flat, savory pie made by wrapping layers of *warqa*, a thin, flat pastry similar to phyllo, around a filling usually made with a mixture of pigeon meat and eggs flavored with spices and fresh herbs. *B'stila* is a traditional festival dish from Fez.

caid: an Islamic judge.

charmoula: a spice mixture typically used for marinating fish, chicken, and lamb. Recipes vary, but ingredients usually include garlic, fresh cilantro, cumin, paprika, cayenne, olive oil, and occasionally, preserved lemons.

couscous: a staple of the Maghreb made primarily from a mixture of semolina, wheat flour, and water that is shaped into grains ranging from fine to quite coarse. Traditionally, couscous is cooked by soaking in water and steaming in a special steamer called a *couscoussier.* The word *couscous* can also describe a variety of other grains, including barley and millet, cooked in a similar fashion.

djellebah: the traditional hooded robes worn by men and women in Morocco.

Fatima's hand: a representation of a woman's hand found frequently in Moroccan decoration and jewelry. According to legend, when the prophet Mohammed was preparing for battle, his mother, Fatima, whose hand had been freshly painted with henna designs, placed her hand on his shoulder in a farewell gesture, leaving a mark on his skin. When Mohammed was successful in battle, this mark was considered to have been a sign of good luck.

hammam: a bathhouse, traditionally communal and heated by a wood burning stove, where an array of bathing activities take place including vigorous scrubbing, steam-bathing, and washing in hot water.

harissa: a condiment made from pureed hot red peppers and spices that originated in Tunisia.

kasbah: a fortified mud-brick castle, often strategically situated where warlords could control the passage of desert caravans.

kilim: a weft-faced woven rug created by weaving colored weft threads through warp threads. Kilims are made primarily in Morocco, the Caucasus, Turkey, and Afghanistan.

ksar (ksour, plural): a fortified village built of mud bricks.

lmrach: a small bottle, usually made of glass and metal, for dispensing droplets of orange flower water when cleansing hands before and after meals.

Maghreb: the region of North Africa that comprises Morocco, Tunisia, and Algeria.

muezzin: an Islamic prayer leader who delivers the daily calls to prayer from a mosque's minaret.

medina: an ancient walled city.

mousharabiya: decorative wooden screens originally designed to hide the women of Moroccan houses from curious eyes while allowing the women to look out and take the air. They are made by fitting together, without glue, pieces of wood that have been turned and carved.

palmeraie: a date palm grove.

pasha: the chief governing officer of a city or region.

pisé: an ancient building material made of pounded red earth reinforced with straw used for building walls and other structures.

riad: a dwelling built around a square courtyard.

salon marocain: a long, narrow room with banquettes arranged along the walls. This room can be used solely for entertaining or, more traditionally, as a multipurpose space for entertaining and sleeping.

souk: a shop where craftspeople practice traditional crafts and sell their products. *The souks* refers to an area within a medina, or old walled city, where many craftspeople work and sell their products.

sultan: the religious and political leader of a country.

tadlekt: a polished plaster surface that is impermeable to moisture, which was originally used in the *hammam* and underground irrigation canals. *Tadlekt* is created by applying to a surface a coating of powdered limestone plaster to which dry pigment is added for color. When dry, the plaster is rubbed with flat river stones to smooth and harden it. The surface is sealed with egg white, then polished with an oil-based soap that accentuates the color of the pigmented plaster and adds a level of sheen. Several weeks after the soap has been applied, a final layer of wax is applied and the *tadlekt* is polished once more.

tagguebbast: a decorative plaster treatment, also called wet carved plaster, primarily employed for window and door surrounds and cornice moldings. *Tagguebbast* is created by applying a layer of plaster to a wall or ceiling. While the plaster is still damp and somewhat soft, an artisan uses small chisels and other instruments to incise a complex geometric or calligraphic pattern into the surface.

tagine: a stew of meat and/or vegetables that is cooked slowly over a charcoal brazier in an earthenware dish with a conical lid, also called a *tagine*.

Tuareg: African people who have lived in the deserts and mountains of Algeria since prehistoric times.

warqa: a thin, flat pastry similar to phyllo that is used in the preparation of sweet and savory Moroccan dishes. The name derives from the Arabic word for *leaf*, similarly to the word *phyllo*, which derives from the Greek word for *leaf*.

zellij: a mosaic-like decorative surface made by piecing together cut fragments of glazed tile in geometric designs.

Shopping Guide 〜

Note: Country codes have been given for all countries with the exception of the United States. If calling the United States from outside the country, use the country code (1). If you experience difficulty using the numbers provided, please contact your long distance operator for assistance.

Featured Furniture, Textile, and Design Studios

Valérie Barkowski

Contemporary linens
www.vbarkowski.com
www.miazia.com

Charlotte Barkowski

Contemporary ceramics
www.miazia.com

Taoufiq Baroudi

Contemporary textiles, linens, and clothing
54, Derb Hammam
40000 Mouassine, Marrakech
Telephone: 212 01 17 36 56
Fax: 212 04 44 15 68
tbaroudi@hotmail.com

Frederic Butz Design

Contemporary metal furniture
3 Derb Riad
La Kasbah
Marrakech

Telephone: 212 55 38 36 33
Fax: 212 44 43 17 86

La Cour des Myrtes

Furniture and interior design
Michel Durand-Meyrier
Jérôme Vermelin
28 Derb El Hammam, Isbtienne
Marrakech
Telephone: 212 44 38 09 49
Fax: 212 44 38 09 43
www.mezouar.com
info@mezouar.com

Annie Kelly

2074 Watsonia Terrace
Los Angeles, CA 90068
Telephone: 323-549-0121
streetkelly@earthlink.net

Luciano Monti

Contemporary furniture
Centre Commercial Villa Vista
9000 Tanger
Fax: 212(0)39 94 1977 ·
Mobile telephone: 212(0)61 34 43 96
www.lucianomonti.ma
l.monti@iam.net.ma

Paige Hathaway Thorn

Hand-dyed and screened silks
www.paigehathawaythorn.com
info@paigehathawaythorn.com

The boutique at Mô Tea Room on Heddon Street in London

Shopping in Essaouira

L'Art de Goulmim
Large selection of Moroccan carpets
11, Rue Laâlouj
Essaouira
Telephone: 212 44 47 59 81

Mohamed Badra
Antique jewelry, vintage ceramics, and an eclectic array of decorative objects
44 Derb Laâlouj, Scala
Essaouira
Telephone/Fax: 212 44 47 51 50
http.badra.antiques.free.fr
momo_badrao@hotmail.com

Chez Les Hommes Bleus
Antique carved wooden artifacts, leather crafts, jewelry, and more
19 Rue Skala
Essaouira
Telephone: 212 44 47 54 60

La Caverne d'Ali Baba
Berber and Tuareg jewelry, textiles, and crafts
26 Place El Khaîma
Essaouira
Telephone: 212 0 62 09 42 37

Galerie Jama El Boussaidi
Traditional Moroccan crafts
22 Rue Ibnou Rochd
(near Hôtel les Ramparts)
Essaouria
Telephone: 212 44 78 48 97

Taros
Gallery of contemporary art and crafts
Place Moulay Hassan
Essaouira
Telephone: 212 44 47 64 07
Fax: 212 44 47 64 08

Shopping in Fez

Abbad Andaloussi/Abdess Alam
A traditional wood-painting studio and gallery
12 Sidi Ahmed Shewi
Rue Siege
Fez

L'Art de Tissage
Traditional and contemporary Moroccan textiles
18 Derb Touile
Quartier Lablida
Fez
Telephone: 212 55 63 52 30

L'Art Islamique
An exceptional selection of antique decorative arts and jewelry
36, Derb Touil
Fez
Telephone/Fax: 212 55 74 12 04
www.artislamique.co.ma
artislamique@artislamique.co.ma

Maison Mabrouka
Traditional Moroccan carpets
11, Derb Mechatte
Derb Touil Blida
Fez
Telephone: 212 55 74 17 84
mabroukazidine@hotmail.com

Terasse des Tanneurs

Traditional and contemporary leather crafts

2, Chouara Lablida

Fez

Telephone: 212 55 74 08 42

Tissage du Costume National

Traditional Moroccan textiles

8, Derb Touil

Blida Quarter

Fez

Telephone: 212 55 63 52 63

azamitissage@hotmail.com

Shopping in Marrakech

Amanjena

The Amanjena resort's boutique with contemporary and traditional tableware, clothing, jewelry, and decorative items

Route de Ouarzazate, km 12

Marrakech Palmeraie

Telephone: 212 44 40 33 53

Fax: 212 44 40 34 77

Beldi

Contemporary textiles for the home and for wear designed by Taoufiq Baroudi

9–11 Souikat Laksour

Marrakech

Telephone: 212 44 44 10 76

Mustapha Blaoui

A treasure trove of traditional crafts and carpets

142/144 Arset Aouzale

Bab Doukkala

Marrakech

Telephone: 212 44 38 52 40

Fax: 212 44 37 60 15

Tresordesnomades@hotmail.com

Chey-Lahbila Abdou

Antique crafts and leather

Souk Mijjarine

Souk Lakbir 93

Marrakech

Telephone: 212 44 44 00 82

Comptoir Darna

Contemporary Moroccan designs for the home and for wear (located behind the restaurant of the same name)

Avenue Echouhada

Hivernage, Marrakech

Telephone: 212 44 43 77 02

Fax: 212 44 44 77 47

comptoirdarna@iam.net.ma

Galerie L'Art Arabe

Antique Moroccan crafts

75, Souika Mouassine

Marrakech

Telephone: 212 44 44 39 19

Fax: 212 44 44 22 93

Ministero del Gusto

A contemporary art and design gallery including furniture, lighting, artwork, and interior design services

22 Derb el Mouassine

Marrakech

Telephone: 212 44 42 64 55

Fax: 212 44 42 79 36

mingusto@iam.net.ma

L'Orientaliste

Traditional and contemporary designs for the home

11 and 15 Rue de la Liberté

Marrakech

Telephone: 212 44 43 40 74

Fax: 212 44 43 04 43

orientaliste@wanadoo.net.ma

Le Petit Palais

A large selection of fine antique and contemporary Moroccan carpets
3 Derb El Messfioui
Znikt Rahba El Kdima
Marrakech
Telephone: 212 44 39 14 83
Fax: 212 44 39 14 86

Ryad Tamsna

Contemporary designs for home and wear including designs by Meryanne Loum-Martin, an art gallery, and a restaurant
Riad Zitoun Jdid
23, Derb Zanka Daika
Marrakech
Telephone: 212 44 38 52 72
Fax: 212 44 38 52 71
www.tamsna.com
info@tamsna.com

Shopping in New York

Imports from Marrakech

Lamps, *zellij*-topped tables, tea glasses, and more
88 Tenth St.
New York, NY 10011
Telephone: 212-675-9700
Fax: 212-242-2319

Mosaic House

Moroccan tiles and *zellij*-ornamented furniture
62 West 22nd St.
New York, NY 10010
Telephone: 212-414-2525
Fax: 212-414-2526
www.mosaichse.com

Shopping in Los Angeles

Kenza

Moroccan furniture, lamps, and small decorative objects
612 South La Brea Ave.
Los Angeles, CA 90036
Telephone: 323-930-1768
Fax: 323-930-9438
www.kenzaimports.com

Indigo Seas

An eclectic selection of antiques and home decorative objects including Moroccan designs
123 North Robertson Blvd.
Los Angeles, CA 90048
Telephone: 310-550-8758
Fax: 310-550-6939

Shopping in Martha's Vineyard

Gogo Maroc

Moroccan rugs, tents, lanterns, home furnishings, fabrics, clothing, and contemporary jewelry
Beach St. Ext.
Vineyard Haven, MA 02568
Telephone/Fax: 508-693-0117
www.gogojewelry.com
gogo@gogojewelry.com

Shopping on St. Simons, Georgia

Gogo

Moroccan rugs, tents, lanterns, home furnishings, fabrics, clothing, and contemporary jewelry
600 Sea Island Road, Suite 6
St. Simons, GA 31522
Telephone/Fax: 912-634-8875
www.gogojewelry.com
gogo@gogojewelry.com

Shopping Outside Washington, DC

Nomad and Medina

Baskets, tile top tables, ceramics, lanterns, and screens as well as Moroccan-inspired clothing made in Morocco
8865 Monard Dr.
Silver Spring, MD 20910
Telephone: 301-495-2700
Showroom open by appointment
www.moroccanbaskets.com
medinanomad@aol.com

Shopping in London

Frontiers

Antique and tribal jewelry, old Moroccan amber and silver beads
37–9 Pembridge Rd.
London W11
Telephone: 44(0)20 7727 6132

Mô Tea Room

Antique and contemporary Moroccan crafts and decorative objects
23 Heddon St.
London W1
Telephone: 44(0)20 7734 3999

Spitafields Market

Contemporary Moroccan textiles, slippers, and decorative objects, open Sundays in the covered market
Commercial St.
London E1
Telephone: 44(0)20 7247 6590

Shopping in Paris

Boutique Regina Rubens

Decorative objects from Morocco and inspired by Morocco
15, rue Pavee (4eme Arrondissement)
Telephone: 33(0)1 44 54 07 04

Caravane

Twentieth century designs from Morocco and beyond
6, rue Pavee (4eme Arrondissement)
Telephone: 33(0)1 44 61 06 20
www.caravane.fr

Epicerie-Souk Midi-Minuit

Moroccan accessories for wear and Moroccan groceries
14, rue Surmelin (20eme Arrondissement)
Telephone: 33(0)6 63 21 52 29

La Grande Mosquee de Paris

Tearoom, Moroccan spa, and boutique with Moroccan decorative accessories
2, place Puits de l'Ermite (5eme Arrondissement)
Telephone: 33(0)1 45 35 97 33
Fax: 33(0)1 45 35 16 23

Mia Zia

Contemporary and traditional Moroccan textiles, ceramics, clothing, and decorative accessories
4, rue de Caumartin (9eme Arrondissement)
Telephone: 33(0)1 44 51 95 45
www.miazia.com
stores@miazia.net

Reflets d'Orient

An oriental bazaar with furniture, *tagines*, jewelry, and more
142, rue de Rennes (6eme Arrondissement)
Telephone: 33(0)1 45 48 77 98
Fax: 33(0)1 40 49 05 82

Shopping Online

Berber Imports

Moroccan lamps, ceramics, chests, furniture, rugs, jewelry, clothing, and more
Main office and warehouse address:
Atlanta Metropolitan
9467 Main St., Suite 120
Woodstock, GA 30188
Telephone: 770-926-1900
Fax: 877-277-7227
www.berberimports.com

The Kilim Warehouse

Large selection of Moroccan rugs, available in store or online
Galicia, Spain
Mobile telephone: 44(0)7836 225048
www.kilim-warehouse.co.uk

Moroccan Design Imports

Traditional furnishings, home accessories, antiques, tents, iron window grills, painted shutters, and more
1431 S. Robertson Blvd.
Los Angeles, CA 90035
Telephone: 310-278-7662
and 443 E. Broadway
Long Beach, CA 90802
Telephone: 562-212-9866
www.moroccandesignimports.com

Le Souk

Arts and crafts of the Mediterranean, including contemporary styles of iron chairs and tables from Morocco and *zellij* tabletops
The Partner One Corp.
443-B Tecate Rd., #448
Tecate, CA 91980
Telephone: 805-782-4074 or 619-839-3655
www.lesouk.com

Shopping for Cookware and Special Ingredients

London

Le Marrakech Food Store

Moroccan groceries
64 Golborne Rd., W10
Telephone: 44(0)20 8964 8307

Le Maroc Halal Meat Supermarket

Halal meats, Moroccan spices and special ingredients
94 Golborne Rd., W10
Telephone: 44(0)20 8968 9783

The Spice Shop

A selection of Moroccan spices
1 Blenheim Crescent, W11
Telephone: 44(0)20 7221 4448
www.thespiceshop.co.uk

Paris

Epicerie-Souk Midi-Minuit

Moroccan accessories for wear and Moroccan groceries
14, rue Surmelin (20eme Arrondissement)
Telephone: 33(0)6 63 21 52 29

New York

Kalustyan's

Moroccan condiments, olives, and more
123 Lexington Ave.
New York, NY 10016
Telephone: 212-685-3451
www.kalustyans.com
sales@kalustyans.com

Zabar's
Moroccan condiments, olives, and more
2245 Broadway
New York, NY 10024
Telephone: 212-496-1234 or 800-697-6301
www.zabars.com

Online Sources in America

Ameerah Imports
In addition to traditional Moroccan furnishings, decorative objects, and accessories, this online shop offers a wide range of Moroccan spices and condiments and cooking tools including *tagines* and *couscoussieres*.
Telephone: 800-860-7341
www.ameerahimports.com

Le Creuset
Cast-iron *tagine* with earthenware lid
Telephone: 877-273-8738
www.lecreuset.com

Sur La Table
Le Creuset *tagine,* tea glasses, Moroccan serving dishes, and more
Telephone: 800-243-0852
www.surlatable.com

Places to Stay in Morocco

Amanjena
Route de Ouarzazate, km 12
Marrakech 40000
Telephone: 212 44 40 33 53
Fax: 212 44 40 34 77
www.amanresorts.com
amanjena@cybernet.net.ma

Les Deux Tours
Douar Abiad, Marrakech
Telephone: 212 44 32 95 27
Fax: 212 44 32 95 23
www.deux-tours.com
deuxtours@iam.net.ma

CaravanSerai
Ouled Ben Rahmoune, Marrakech
Telephone: 212 44 30 03 02
Fax: 212 44 30 02 62
www.caravanserai-marrakesh.com
caravanserai@iam.net.ma

Dar Noor Charana
31 Derb el Kébir, Marrakech
Telephone: 212 44 38 60 94
Fax: 212 44 38 69 31
Noorcharana@iam.net.ma

Dar Kawa
Marrakech Medina
102, Dar El Bacha
Telephone: 212 44 42 91 33
Fax: 212 44 39 10 71
Marrakech.medina@iam.net.ma
www.marrakech-medina.com

Dar Tamsna
Marrakech Palmeraie
Telephone: 212 44 32 93 40
Fax: 212 44 32 98 84
www.tamsna.com
info@tamsna.com

El Cherquï

Vicinity of Essaouira

www.essaouirahomescollection.com

Jnane Tamsna

Marrakech Palmeraie

Telephone: 212 44 38 52 72

Fax: 212 44 38 52 72

www.tamsna.com

info@tamsna.com

La Maison Bleue

2, Place de l'Istiqlal, Batha

Fez

Telephone/Fax: 212 55 74 18 43 or

212 55 74 06 86

www.maisonbleue.com

resa@maisonbleue.com

Riad 72

72 Arset Awzel

Marrakech

Telephone: 212 44 38 7629

www.riad72.com

riad.72@wanadoo.net.ma

Riyad El Cadi

59, Derb El Cadi

Marrakech

Telephone: 212 44 37 86 55

Fax: 212 44 37 84 78

www.riyadelcadi.com

riyadelcadi@iam.net.ma

Riyad El Mezouar

28 Derb El Hammam, Issebtinne

Marrakech 40000

Telephone: 212 44 38 09 49

Fax: 212 44 38 09 43

www.mezouar.com

info@mezouar.com

Riad Enija

Derb Mesfioui, no. 9

Marrakech

Telephone: 212 44 44 09 26

Fax: 212 44 44 27 00

www.riadenija.com

Riadenija@cybernet.net.ma

Riad Kaiss

65, Derb Jdid

Marrakech

Telephone/Fax: 212 44 44 01 41

www.riadkaiss.com

riad@riadkaiss.com

Riad Mabrouka

56, Derb El Bahia

Riad Zitoun Jdid

Marrakech

Telephone/Fax: 212 44 37 75 79

www.riad-mabrouka.com

info@riad-mabrouka.com

Villa Argana

Vicinity of Essaouira

Telephone: 212 44 47 34 83

Telephone: 212 44 47 43 65

http://freespace.virgin.net/villa.argana

Agrgw@aol.com

Travel Services

The Classic Safari Company
Private, custom tours of Morocco and other African destinations.
Telephone: 61 2 9327 0666
Fax: 61 2 9327 0667
156 Queen St., Woollahra, NSW 2025 Australia
www.classicsafaricompany.com.au
Julie@classicsafaricompany.com.au

Diversity Excursions, Ltd.
An organization offering a wide range of tours exploring the culture, ecology, and history of southern Morocco. All proceeds benefit the Global Diversity Foundation, a charitable organization that sponsors training and research on agricultural, biological and cultural diversity.
Fax: 212 44 32 98 84
info@tamsna.com

Heritage Tours
Private, custom designed in-depth tours of Morocco tailored to a variety of interests and travel styles.
121 West 27th St., Suite 1201
New York, NY 10001
Telephone: 212-206-8400
Or 800-378-4555
Fax: 212-206-9101
www.heritagetoursONLINE.com
info@heritagetoursONLINE.com

Private World
Private luxury villas in Moroccan locations including Tangiers, Marrakech, Asylah, and Skoura.
46 A Harrowby St.
London W1 H 5HT
Telephone: 44 207 723 55 99
Fax: 44 207 723 55 51
www.privateworldvillas.com
info@privateworldvillas.com

Royal Air Maroc
The only airline offering non-stop service from the U.S. and Canada to Casablanca with brand-new flight equipment featuring the latest modern fleet of Boeing 767s and three classes of service: first, business, and coach. The winner of several Boeing and FAA safety awards, Royal Air Maroc also offers flights linking Morocco with the Middle East, Europe, and other points in Africa and an extensive domestic schedule of flights to all major points of interest within Morocco.
55 East 59th St., Suite 17B
New York, NY 10022-1112
Telephone: 800-344-6726
info@royalairmaroc.com
www.royalairmaroc.com

Moroccan National Tourism Office
Information about traveling in Morocco, including destinations, climate and distances, domestic transportation, accommodations, and dining.
20 W. 46th St., Suite 1201
New York, NY 10017
Telephone: 212-557-2520
mntonyonmt@aol.com
www.tourism-in-morocco.com

Index ⌒~⌒

Abbadi, Mehdi and Kenza El, 56, 58, 60
absinthe tea, 156
Achat, Karim El, 81
Alaoui, Rita, 180
Amanjena, 108–16
Andalusian style, 24, 45, 46, 99
  Glaoui Palace, 18, 33, 155–59
  hallmarks of, 18, 24, 51, 56–58, 177
    La Maison Bleue, 56–64
    Riad Enija, 148, 151
    Riad Mabrouka, 133–137
Angell, Stephen, 124, 130
art deco, 12, 15, 25, 27, 28, 45, 56, 58, 71, 181

Ballard, Glen and Liv, 187–88, 191
Barkowski, Charlotte, 38, 104, 107
Barkowski, Valérie, 102, 107
Baroudi, Taoufiq, 41
Bartels, Herwig, 65–71
bassin, 108, 112, 210
Berber, 23, 27, 28, 34, 42, 45, 70, 130, 134, 147, 170, 201, 206, 210
Bizzarri, Fabrizio, 162, 165–68
Boccara, Charles, 27, 28, 29, 37
Boccara, Mathieu, 27, 28
Bouamrani, Reda, 120
Bouftila, Mohammed, 156
Boukhars, Abdelkhalek, 155–56, 159
Brichambaut, Arielle de, 38, 54
Bridger, Nancy, 124–32
Butz, Frederic, 42, 102, 104

caid, 151, 210
calligraphy, 24, 33, 40, 202

CaravanSerai, 27, 28
charmoula, 96, 210
Chiche, Marcel, 72–80
Church, Stuart, 18, 140, 143, 144, 147
Cinel, Giovanna, 81–86
Coerding, Björn, 151
Comptoir Darna (Marrakech), 72–80
couscous, 61–62, 170, 210
cuisine, 93, 99, 112–13, 170, 172, 181–82, 210, 211. See also recipes

Dar Andalusia (Los Angeles), 187–92
Dar Kawa (Marrakech), 38, 101–7
Dar Noor Charana (Marrakech), 34
Dar Tamsna (Marrakech outskirts), 12, 15, 25, 27, 38, 40, 46–55
delirium, 31, 138–215
Deltour, Philippe, 120
Dianda, Elisabeth, 34
djellebah, 102, 124, 210
Dogon architecture, 165, 166
Durand-Meyrier, Michel, 30, 41, 193–97

El Cherquï (Essaouira), 124–32
Essaouira, 20, 124, 127, 205, 206, 207

Fathy, Hassan, 169
Fatima's hand, 102, 210
Ferguson, Gogo, 87–93
Ferre, Christian, 198–204
Fez, 18, 20, 56, 139, 155–61
Foley, Annie, 93
French Protectorate, 12, 19, 25, 45, 134, 181, 190, 193, 197
fusion, 31, 44–96, 118, 123, 134, 181, 182, 193, 194

Gaudi, Antonio, 165
geometric patterns, 13, 24, 99, 181. See also zellij
Glaoui, Thami El, 134, 139, 155, 159

Glaoui Palace (Fez), 18, 155–61
Gogo Maroc (Martha's Vineyard), 87–97
Gwatkin, Andy, 205–7

Haldimann, Ursula, 151, 152
hammam, 27, 210
harissa, 94, 210
Hispano-Muslim style. *See* Andalusian style

Islamic patterns, 24, 70, 72, 123

Jelloun, Ben, 156, 159
Jnane Tamsna (Marrakech outskirts), 117–23
Jones, Barnaby, 112–13

Kadiri, Jaouad, 16, 140–47
kasbah, 23, 28, 45, 46, 99, 108, 210
Kelly, Annie, 188, 191
Kemia Bar (London), 169, 172

La Maison Bleue (Fez), 56–64
Lippini, Alessandra, 162, 165–68
Lmrach, 169, 210–11
London, 169–75
Los Angeles, 187–92
Loum-Martin, Meryanne, 12–14, 25, 27, 40, 46–55, 117–23,
    178–82

Mali, 162, 165, 166
Mamounia Hotel, 25, 194
Marrakech, 12, 13, 20, 25, 28, 33, 46, 65, 72, 76, 81, 101,
    112, 133, 134, 148, 151, 165, 191, 193, 198
Martha's Vineyard, 87–88, 93
Martin, Gary, 13, 117–18, 123
Maxwell, Gavin, 139
Mazouz, Mourad (Momo), 169–72
McKeel, Michael, 188
medina, 101, 178, 193, 198, 211

minimalism, 31, 38, 98–137, 194
Ministero del Gusto (Marrakech), 162–68
mint tea, 13, 107, 113, 155, 156
    recipe, 159
Momo Restaurant Familial (London), 169–75
Monti, Luciano, 42
Moorish revival, 20, 23, 45, 187–92
Mô Tea Room (London), 169, 172, 173
mousharabiya, 58, 133, 134, 144, 170, 198, 201, 211
Mouyal, Elie, 28

Naldi, Nadir, 162, 165
Néri, Pierre-Jean and Catherine, 133–37

Orientalists, 13, 16, 19, 20, 23, 29, 45, 72, 76, 140, 147,
    172, 173, 193–97
Ourad, Mohamed, 170

palmeraie, 12, 46, 118, 140, 211
Palmeraie Villa (Marrakech outskirts), 140–47
pisé, 28, 45, 112, 211
Price, Roy Seldon, 187

Quartermaine, Carolyn, 151, 152

recipes, 61–63, 77–79, 94–97, 113–15, 159–60, 174–75,
    183–85
  Basil-Olive Tapenade, 78
  Briouats of Goat Cheese, Sun-Dried Tomatoes, and
    Cilantro, 183
  B'stila (Mock Pigeon Pie), 160
  Charmoula Sauce, 96
  Chicken in a Green Herb Sauce, 61
  Chicken with Gingery Fruit Sauce, 184
  Couscous of the Thirteenth Century, 61–62
  Eggplant Caviar, 79
  Gingery Fruit Sauce, 184–85
  Herbed Tomato Sauce, 184

Marinated Fish with Fried Vermicelli, 78–79

Mock Polenta Stars with Moroccan Tomato Chutney, Chevre, and Mint, 94–95

Moroccan Mint Tea, 159

Moroccan Tomato Chutney, 95

New Potato Ragout with Olives, 115

Orange and Date Salad, 115

Pastilla with Milk Custard, 59, 62–63

Pesto Couscous with Pan-Fried Scallops and Rock Shrimp with Red Pepper Coulis, 175

Poached Pears with Moroccan Spices, 185

Preserved Lemons, 113

Saffron-Scented Tagine of Potato, Okra, Green Beans, and Sweet Corn, 96–97

Scallop Brochettes with Charmoula Sauce, 96

Seared Red Mullet with Charmoula Paste, 114

Seared Tuna with Fried Eggplant and Mixed Pepper Confit, 174

Sexy Drink, The, 77

Spicy Harissa Mussels in the Shell, 94

repose, 31, 176–209

riad, 68, 101–2, 133, 134, 178, 191, 211

Riad 72 (Marrakech), 33, 81–86

Riad Enija (Marrakech), 20, 41, 148–54

Riad Kaiss (Marrakech), 198–204

Riad Mabrouka (Marrakech), 133–37

Riyad El Cadi (Marrakech), 37, 65–71

Riyad El Mezouar (Marrakech), 29, 30, 193–97

Ryad Tamsna (Marrakech), 15, 178–86

Saccomanno, Chantal, 152

Sadek, Fouad, 67

salon marocain, 58, 172, 197, 201, 211

Salvoni, Pier Lorenzo, 151

Sayre, David, 87–93

Siméon, Christophe, 134

souk, 12, 101, 211

Strauss, Micol, 206–7

tableware, 34, 38, 54, 104, 107, 112, 159

tadlekt, 25, 27, 28, 34, 51, 72, 81, 82, 118, 123, 136, 144, 166, 172, 201, 211

tagguebbast. See wet-carved plaster

tagine, 59, 96–97, 107, 211

tea service, 107, 155, 156, 159

Thorn, Paige Hathaway, 6, 40, 213

Tuareg, 133, 134, 211

Tuttle, Ed, 108, 112

Vermelin, Jérôme, 30, 41, 193–97

Villa Argana (Ghazouna), 205–9

warqa, 181, 211

wet-carved plaster, 24, 25, 85, 159, 162, 211

Wilbaux, Quentin, 68, 101

Willis, Bill, 27, 28, 29, 33

Yacout (Marrakech), 25, 28, 33

Zecha, Adrian, 108

zellij, 25, 27, 28, 33, 50, 56, 58, 67, 68, 70, 99, 144, 151, 159, 162, 177, 201, 202, 211

New Moroccan Style
DESIGN – 2 – Morocco
NE-90